NORTH CAROLINA
STATE BOARD OF COMMUNITY COLLEGES
LIBRARIES
ASHEVILLE-BUNCOMBE TECHNICAL COMMUNITY COLLEGE

Y0-CSS-218

DISCARDED

AUG 6 2025

U.S.- Japan Relations:
An Agenda for the Future

**edited by
Ronald A. Morse**

UNIVERSITY PRESS OF AMERICA

Lanham • New York • London

PACIFIC ✦ FORUM

Copyright © 1989 by

Pacific Forum
University Press of America,® Inc.

4720 Boston Way
Lanham, MD 20706

3 Henrietta Street
London WC2E 8LU England

All rights reserved

Printed in the United States of America

British Cataloging in Publication Information Available

The contributors to this volume have expressed their
views as private citizens.

Co–published by arrangement with Pacific Forum.

"Japanese–American Defense Policies
for a Post–Reagan Era" © 1989 by
John Endicott

Library of Congress Cataloging-in-Publication Data

U.S.–Japan relations : an agenda for the future / edited by Ronald A. Morse.
p. cm.
Background papers for a meeting of the Japanese–American Study
Committee on Comprehensive Security held 4/88 and sponsored by the
Pacific Forum.
1. United States– –Foreign relations– –Japan. 2. Japan– –Foreign
relations– –United States. I. Morse, Ronald A. II. Pacific Forum.
III. Japanese–American Study Committee on Comprehensive Security.
IV. Title: United States–Japan relations. V. Title: US–Japan relations.
E183.8.J3U17   1989   88–36667 CIP
327.73052– –dc19
ISBN 0–8191–7348–7 (alk. paper)
ISBN 0–8191–7349–5 (pbk. : alk. paper)

All University Press of America books are produced on acid-free paper.
The paper used in this publication meets the minimum requirements of American
National Standard for Information Sciences—Permanence of Paper for Printed Library
Materials, ANSI Z39.48-1984.   ∞

Contents

Foreword
Lloyd R. Vasey — *v*

Introduction
Ronald A. Morse — *vii*

"Formulating an American Agenda for Asia"
Robert A. Scalapino — *1*

"A Japanese Agenda for Asian Politics and Security"
Seizaburo Sato — *15*

"The Economics of U.S.-Japan Relations in the Asia-Pacific Region"
Edward Lincoln — *25*

"Reorienting the Japanese Economy for the Future"
Yutaka Kosai — *45*

"Japanese-American Defense Policies for a Post-Reagan Era"
John Endicott — *51*

Committee Participants — *67*

FOREWORD

This report, reflecting the ideas and advice of the Japanese-American Study Committee on Comprehensive Security, is one of several projects by the Pacific Forum to bring wider attention to critical issues focused on the Asia-Pacific region. This particular project brought together private sector and government leaders for candid discussions about the political, economic and security issues that today challenge the leadership in Tokyo and Washington and will form the basis for relations in the 1990s.

The U.S.-Japan relationship has emerged as the free world's most important bilateral relationship from the standpoint of economics and politics and increasingly security as well. Together, the two countries can make unparalleled contributions to global peace, stability and economic development. Operating independently, neither can successfully address the issues facing the future of the Pacific Basin community. Together and in cooperation they can have a major impact. While the bilateral economic tensions and political uncertainties often seem to threaten the promise of this relationship, the forces for overcoming them are increasingly positive.

The benefits of coordination and cooperation can come only if American and Japanese leaders turn current problems to their long-term mutual advantage by renewing their political commitment to work together and strengthen all aspects of their relationship. Five participants in the Japanese-American Study Committee on Comprehensive Security have written essays for this volume with those goals in mind—the goals

Pacific Forum

of putting reality into perspective and suggesting modest, but visionary recommendations for the future.

These essays and the recommendations in them are a first step in creating a framework for a more comprehensive and mutually reinforcing relationship between Tokyo and Washington for the future. In order to live and work together creatively, the United States and Japan must develop a shared vision of their future and a set of institutional arrangements that broaden and deepen the complex bilateral interdependence that already binds them.

The creative engagement that is emphasized here requires a firmer awareness of shared strategic and economic objectives in order to maximize the combined strength of both nations. There is a sense that both sides have taken the U.S.-Japan relationship for granted for too long and that despite current tensions, we now stand on the threshold of an opportunity to reinforce the centrality of this relationship.

The committee conference held in April 1988 and this report were made possible by grants from The Pew Charitable Trusts, the Sequoia Foundation and The John D. and Catherine T. MacArthur Foundation; and through the cooperation of the Asia Pacific Association of Japan. Many people contributed to the success of this project, but three individuals in particular, Maura Fujihira, Marie Lawrie and Gail Uyetake of Pacific Forum, deserve special mention for their administrative skills in helping prepare this report.

To the committee participants who so freely shared their ideas, suggestions, and hard work, we express our sincere thanks.

L. R. Vasey
President
Pacific Forum

Introduction

     This book is about the implications of change—fairly rapid change in Japan in the economic, political and strategic areas and much slower and slightly less impressive change in America. The focus of the essays here is on how these changes relate to the strength and vitality of the U.S.-Japan relationship and what the likely scenarios are for effective cooperation in the Pacific Basin during the 1990s. The emphasis throughout the book is on the current trends and future implications of the policies now being implemented on both sides. The overall tone of the volume is one of cautious optimism.

     The essays included here deal with the domestic political agendas in both Japan and America. They also address the economic trends in both countries and how cooperative defense issues are shaping up for the future. Overall the authors feel that the prospects are good for continued successful relations, but warning flags are raised for consideration where appropriate. What is special about this set of essays is that the authors here make fresh recommendations for policies and institutional arrangements that go beyond earlier ideas on how to improve the U.S.-Japan relationship.

     The authors do not get into abstract cooperative schemes like *Pax Americana II*, *Pax Nipponica* or the half-way idea of *Pax Ameripponica*. Likewise, they do not revive old approaches (wisemen groups) in slightly refurbished form. Instead, they have practical proposals that address

Pacific Forum

serious issues in concrete ways. I will discuss some of these proposals later in the introduction.

The essays in this volume were the background papers for a two-day meeting of the Japanese-American Study Committee on Comprehensive Security which met in April 1988. The meeting was sponsored by the Pacific Forum. The purpose was to assess the major political, economic, and security issues confronting the United States and Japan in the Asia-Pacific region, and to propose policy recommendations that Tokyo and Washington might undertake to improve the overall effectiveness of their cooperative planning and consultation. While this introduction will attempt to summarize the full range of discussions by the committee members, the papers included here are important because they formed the substantive basis for the discussions.

The committee met against the backdrop of growing challenges to the U.S.-Japan relationship, particularly in the trade and technology areas. While some of those issues have dropped from the headlines new issues continually surface. There was agreement then (and now) that the U.S.-Japanese relationship is the cornerstone of Asia-Pacific regional stability and prosperity and that even better cooperation between Tokyo and Washington could have an overall positive impact for the region as a whole. Thus, the region's steady economic development and the continued deterrence of major threats to peace create enormous opportunities for the U.S.-Japanese economic, political and security relationship. Enhancing the existing strength and vitality of this relationship through new mechanisms, the committee concluded, remained the essential prerequisite for sustaining economic growth and stability throughout the region.

Asia demands the coordination of U.S.-Japan relations that the committee participants recognized. The political democratization process in Taiwan and South Korea requires a stable Asian environment. America's strategic presence in Northeast Asia allows for the sustained economic growth already underway. Japanese foreign aid will bolster U.S. ties with the Philippines. A continuation of smooth China-Hong Kong-Taipei relations will enhance peace in Indochina. Japan's Southeast Asian economic base in Indonesia, Thailand, Burma and elsewhere ensures a stable political transition. America's continued ties in the South Pacific will dampen Soviet adventurism. And not unimportantly, growth and prosperity in the Pacific will provide markets for American products and help to balance regional trade flows.

New eras require, in the eyes of the committee participants, new methods. The past decade has witnessed a profound change in the relative position of the two countries in the world economy, with the United States now the largest debtor nation and Japan the largest creditor. At the same

Introduction

time, the huge imbalance in U.S.-Japanese trade and the growing Japanese technological challenge to American industry have generated pressures and tensions that are testing the viability and sustainability of the relationship. The U.S.-Japanese relationship has never been more interdependent than at present, yet increasing nationalistic assertiveness and discontent in both countries could undermine the continued success of this interdependence.

During its deliberations in April, the committee drew repeated attention to major political and economic challenges that jointly confront the United States and Japan. Robert Scalapino's essay, included here, provided the framework for this discussion. First, there is the challenge of democratization and increased demands for political participation evident in the region, with Korea and the Philippines being the most prominent cases. Second, there is a mounting geostrategic challenge, with pressures to alter the relative security burdens with allies. Both problem areas will require multilateral solutions, and suggest that the tasks and the opportunities confronting Washington and Tokyo are complex.

The changes underway in the socialist and communist worlds add further to this complexity, and were a central theme in the committee's discussions. There is a growing recognition of the failures of the Marxist models of economic development: China has led the way in this process, but the Soviet Union under Mikhail Gorbachev appears to be reaching comparable conclusions. The implications for these debates and changes are likely to have profound internal and external consequences in Asia, as socialist economies undertake the wrenching task of reforming their domestic economies while also seeking to expand their role in the international system.

Seizaburo Sato's essay links these issues of politics with security in regional planning. The steady growth of Soviet military power in the Asia-Pacific region during the past decade and a half has been a spur to enhanced U.S.-Japan security cooperation. Under Gorbachev, however, the Soviets have evidenced far greater suppleness and sophistication, with a wide-ranging diplomatic offensive intended to seek new opportunities as well as probe for weaknesses in the U.S. political and strategic position. Gorbachev's policies pose a very different security challenge underscoring the need for careful consideration and coordination of U.S. and Japanese policies toward Soviet actions.

Members of the Japanese-American Study Committee on Comprehensive Security were convinced that the future policy agenda confronting Japan and the United States merited more systematic appraisal than it has thus far received on either side of the Pacific. Toward this end, the committee undertook intensive discussions on a wide range of issues, with particular attention to new mechanisms for effective policy coordination. These deliberations lead to the following recommendations, all elaborated on more carefully in the essays included in this volume.

In the area of public policy, the suggestions were mainly in the area of institutional arrangements and better patterns for consultation. The recommendations covered a broad spectrum of issues. Taken together they included a need for:

- Summit meetings between the U.S. President and the Japanese Prime Minister that focus attention on the bilateral relationship and establish deadlines for constructive policies on critical issues. Summits set standards by which the two societies can judge their leaders and should be held annually. As an immediate issue, it will be especially important to hold a summit early in the new U.S. administration and preparations should begin in both Tokyo and Washington immediately after the November U.S. election.
- A common strategic program should be developed through regularized high-level consultations on global security issues and arms control. For this purpose, meetings of Cabinet officers responsible for foreign affairs and defense should be held regularly. Meetings of members of Congress and the Japanese Parliament are also desirable.
- Significant progress in improving bilateral political coordination can also be spurred through the creation of an America-Japan Council. This permanent, non-governmental, bi-national institute, financed with a mix of public-private funds, would anticipate and examine long-term issues and advise government leaders. Members should be chosen for multi-year terms and represent all private constituencies affected by the bilateral relationship.
- Efforts need to be made to coordinate today's bilateral policy consultations as well, with an emphasis on the complex and integrated nature of the U.S.-Japan relationship. For example, regularized consultations should be held on science and technology-related issues, particularly dual-use research and development and the production of sophisticated weapons.
- The broadest possible social and cultural exchange programs to enrich people-to-people contacts should be encouraged and supported. Meetings with a full range of Asian participants should be held as well.

Introduction

Domestic issues, mainly economic in nature, were a major consideration to authors in this volume and were central to the discussions of the committee members during their conference. Ed Lincoln takes a cautious stance on Japan's economic reforms and stresses a careful assessment of past performance as the guide to the future. Yutaka Kosai believes that the economic restructuring going on in Japan now is far more profound than people believe. Together their papers present an excellent assessment of the economic trend lines and prospects for the next few years. The key recommendations by the group in the economic area were:

- Maximize the mutual benefits of changes in exchange rates, with Japan accelerating socio-economic adjustment in line with the Maekawa Reports of 1986 and 1987. Both a Japanese shift from export-oriented growth and a restoration of U.S. economic competitiveness are critical priorities.
- Encourage the reduction of trade barriers throughout the Asia-Pacific region. Japan should continue to improve access to its markets and America must resist the trend toward protectionism.
- Coordinate aid programs more effectively to achieve common political, strategic and economic objectives. The U.S. can and should increase its bilateral economic assistance and Japan must continue to increase its Official Development Assistance (ODA).
- Step up efforts to ensure the success of the Uruguay round of multilateral trade negotiations and cooperate on the resolution of the international debt crisis. Together leaders can and should work together much more effectively to strengthen the international financial system.

The United States in particular should, the participants felt, examine its fiscal policies. Its current account deficit endangers its own economic future and the world's growth prospects. In the short term, the federal budget deficit must be reduced. Over the longer term, today's lopsided imbalance between savings rates and investment must be redressed.

Japan, it was recommended, should continue to promote the expansion of domestic demand in conjunction with U.S. economic adjustments.

The third dimension, regional and global security issues, presented few problems to the group, and most of the committee members thought the current policies were basically sound. The essays here by Sato and John Endicott, while they do suggest areas for basic improvements, agree that

Japan is doing and will continue to do more in the security area. Greater burden sharing is fully recognized. The emphasis in committee talks regarding the future focused on four points:

- The vital importance of the United States-Japan Mutual Security Treaty relationship to Western defense and to peace and stability in East Asia should be reemphasized.
- The U.S. military presence in the Far East and its central role as a peace-keeping force needs reaffirmation.
- The strategic importance of America's military bases in the Western Pacific is undiminished and measures to increase their effectiveness are necessary.
- Japan's current progress in increasing its capabilities to perform roles and missions within the framework of the U.S.-Japanese alliance should be encouraged.

Overall, the members of the Committee on Comprehensive Security thought the implications for the future were straightforward. To strengthen the relationship, the network of official and unofficial ties between the U.S. and Japan must be thickened and better informed. Second, we need a new science of Japanese-American relations that sorts out fact from fiction, economics from psychology and trust from misunderstanding. More evenly balanced relations backed with informed statesmanship must guide all that we do. Finally, while Japan must assume and support greater global strategic cooperation and help in crisis management, this must be pursued in line with its constitutional constraints and guided by the nature of its alliance relationships. All of these points are more fully developed in the essays that follow. Read carefully, they provide a sound foundation for rethinking the fundamentals of U.S.-Japan relations for the decade ahead.

RONALD A. MORSE
Rapporteur and Editor
Development Officer, Office of the Librarian, The Library of Congress. Before that he was Secretary of the Asia Program at the Woodrow Wilson International Center for Scholars in Washington, D.C. Over the past decade he has served in the Departments of State, Defense and Energy in the U.S. Government. Most recently he published, "Japan's Drive to Pre-Eminence," Foreign Policy *(Winter 1987-1988). He has a Ph.D. in Asian Studies from Princeton University.*

Formulating an American Agenda for Asia

Robert A. Scalapino

In each of its dimensions, the American-Japanese relationship today is intimately connected with domestic trends in the two societies. Public attitudes and governmental policies on the home front have always provided the foundations for all foreign policies, but most especially for the vitally important bilateral relations between these two nations.

At the same time, these relations must also be seen in the context of the broader global environment of this extraordinary age. What are its most salient aspects? In recent years, literate people everywhere have been made aware of the information-communications revolution which, together with expanding agricultural-industrial modernization, has posed mankind with a combination of opportunities and problems more complex than in any previous era in human history. On the political-strategic front, meanwhile, it has been commonplace to speak of the loss of American hegemony and the movement from bipolarism to multipolarism.

The Decline of American Hegemony

The capacity—and equally important, the will—of the U.S. to influence global events has declined compared to the situation immediately after World War II. Both failures and successes have contributed to this. American hegemony, however, was never as all-encompassing as some writers seemed to imply, even in that portion of the world where the

Pacific Forum

U.S. sought to exercise its influence. Witness the results of American economic assistance in various parts of Africa and Latin America. Note the stalemate that climaxed the Korean War, and the advent of a communist dictatorship in Cuba. And the list could be extended. On the other hand, "the loss of American hegemony" has not precluded a very large number of states, friendly and otherwise, from continuing to regard America as critical to their futures.

Today, power is unquestionably more widely dispersed than in the past. Yet there are still only two global powers militarily, whatever the limits upon their use of that power. Economically as well, a mere handful of nations determine basic international conditions at present, and foremost among them are the United States and Japan. Indeed, it is from these facts that the signal importance of the U.S.-Japan relation is derived. Other papers in this volume treat the economic and security aspects of this relationship. Granting that no separation can meaningfully be made between various aspects of power, I shall focus upon our political relations. Let me open with some general comments about fundamental political trends within the two societies.

The United States is usually defined as a mature democracy. This is intended to indicate that institutions have been long and deeply implanted that are supportive of the fullest range of freedoms—including genuine political choice by the citizenry—and that also underwrite limitations on the power of government, with an intricate system of checks and balances. Despite these safeguards, voices have been raised on occasion to warn against "an imperial presidency," namely, the acquisition and use of overwhelming power by the chief executive.

Yet it is possible that an opposite threat looms ahead. The factors conducive to division and weakness in the American polity are substantial. Our system permits the executive and legislative branches to be controlled by different parties. Meanwhile, the growing complexities within the executive branch itself, including the proliferation of quasi-independent bodies, have rendered the decision-making process increasingly murky. In Congress, greater "democratization" combined with the absence of party discipline has served to foster an atmosphere of leaderlessness. At the same time, as the case of Speaker James Wright's intervention in dealing with Nicaragua indicated, individual legislators do not hesitate to enter the arena of foreign policy as independent actors.

In the society at large, the citizens' commitment to a given political party is weakening, underwriting the divisive trend. Indeed, cynicism or indifference regarding politics and politicians appears to be growing among the public. At the same time, the influence of interest groups, including single-cause groups, is reaching new heights, a product of refined organizational techniques and ample funds. In addition, the media, particularly the electronic media, vies with government itself in shaping public opinion, without the responsibility of having to state the political predilections of their staffs or treat vital evolutionary developments on a par with that which is sensational.

The greatest challenge confronting all societies in the decades immediately ahead will be to make far-reaching decisions that accord with the requirements of the socioeconomic revolution through which we are passing, and to make them with a timing that matches the tempo of that revolution. This may be especially difficult for democracies since in such societies there is a "natural" decision making process, given the need to cultivate public opinion and develop a degree of consensus. Can that process keep up with the accelerating pace of events? Weak governments, immobilized by the inability to bring disparate groups together or hobbled by internal conflict, will not fare well in the 21st century.

Governance in Japan

The Japanese polity, while more coordinated at present than the United States, appears to be developing some of the trends noted above as "democratization" advances. The dominant party system continues to prevail, but public opinion polls indicate a lessening of firm commitment on the part of the citizenry to any given party including the ruling Liberal Democratic Party (LDP). Within the LDP, leadership is becoming more diffused, with factional governance akin to a corporate board of directors. Meanwhile, the extraordinary influence and power of the bureaucracy—one key to Japan's success in recent decades—are being challenged by increasingly affluent, self-confident and well-organized forces from the private sector. Symbolic of that fact is the increasing role of the professional politician, the political actor whose ties are less to officialdom than to his constituency, and more particularly to a variety of interest groups. Some observers would also argue that interest in politics among the Japanese electorate has declined, as evidenced by lower voter participation.

It is possible to exaggerate signs of divisiveness in Japanese politics. The Liberal Democratic Party still garners the general support of approximately 50 percent of the electorate according to recent opinion polls, and no other party comes close to such support, with the Japan Socialist Party polling only slightly over 10 percent at present. Yet is is clear that the LDP has been inhibited from carrying out certain policies that its principal leaders regard as wise or necessary because it must take into consideration public opinion, or in some cases, powerful interest groups. And whether Japanese leadership be expressive, open and forceful or employ soft, low pressure, consensual tactics, the questions of effective governance and its capacity to guide its society to accept the responsibilities of a major power in the period immediately ahead remain to be tested.

In sum, democratization is not necessarily supportive of internationalism or the optimal timing of decisions that are required even though it may be the least bad system, as Winston Churchill once remarked, especially for advanced industrial societies. There are also cultural factors that affect the attitudes and policies of our two nations. One enters this field with trepidation since casual generalizations, easily made, are often false or misleading. Nonetheless, culture together with historical experience and geopolitical realities go far in shaping attitudes, hence, policy proclivities. Americans, for example, have generally exhibited an impatience with respect to fulfilling assignments, and a distaste for less than total commitments once a task is undertaken. "Get in, get it over with, and get out," is not an uncommon grassroots sentiment, and although many international commitments have been sustained for a considerable length of time, the stretching out of involvements is generally accompanied by a growing unease.

In the aggregate, Americans are outgoing, expansive, and optimistic—and they like optimists as leaders. Generally, they reach out to others, and contacts or friendships are extensive, but vary greatly in intensity or a sense of obligation. As in other dynamic societies, a large majority of Americans believe in their nation and its institutions. Indeed, the superiority of American democracy is generally taken for granted, with the belief that other societies will sooner or later adhere to similar standards. This supports the insistence that a moral foundation underwrite U.S. foreign policy, a factor that differentiates Americans from both Europeans and Asians. And no problem has been more difficult to reconcile than the requirements of American global power and the belief that the United States is and should be morally superior. The American people also have a legacy of generosity, extensive assistance from the private as well as the public sector. This is not only a result of affluence but also of ethics—another facet of American morality.

As participants in a large, heterogeneous society, Americans have had to come to terms with ethnic, religious, and sectional differences, although this task has not been easy nor is it complete. Ethnicity is the one permanent factor in the politics of all societies. Yet as has been implied, most Americans' sense of superiority is not based centrally upon race, but upon system. In recent years, a degree of pessimism has entered American culture, and among millions, religious faith has served as a substitute for secular ideology, a solace in the midst of threats to traditional values.

Robert A. Scalapino

Above all, the United States is a truly revolutionary society at present, with seismic changes occurring that encompass the citizenry as a whole.

As is often emphasized, Japan comes from a very different cultural, historical, and geopolitical background. Once an isolated region on the peripheries of China, Asia's first great civilization, Japan acquired the twin traditions of exclusiveness and adaptation at an early point. If in some degree these are paradoxical traditions, such has been Japan's fate. On the one hand, a unique culture evolved, one basically inward looking, vertically oriented and focused upon the small group, with intensive commitments limited in scope. On the other hand, at points in its history Japan turned out to borrow a written language, religion, political system —and later, technology—always with a talent for shaping foreign innovations to its own character and purposes.

It is understandable that a pervasive sense of ethnicity marks this homogeneous society. Japanese have a stronger sense of their superiority as a *race* than of the superiority of their system, although in some degree, the two meld. Racial consciousness, it might be noted, is powerful throughout Asia, and in heterogeneous societies, represents the single greatest threat to internal political stability as well as a powerful deterrent to regional and international cooperation.

In the case of Japan, as is well known, genuine feelings can be masked, especially when dealing with outsiders. The difference between the dual structure of *honne* (real intent) and *tatemae* (stated intent) has often been noted by Japanese and foreigners alike. Sometimes, this leads to charges of duplicity, just as American casualness in making and changing commitments leads to issues of credibility. Japanese culture, moreover, has made it vastly easier to operate within an hierarchical structure than to deal with relations between equals, a fact of special relevance in the international arena.

Despite the sense of racial superiority implanted in Japanese society, a strain of pessimism has persistently made itself felt among some Japanese, a strain stubbornly resistant until recently to sustained evidence of success. Even today, many Japanese think of themselves as relatively poor, in part the product of constraints on life style due to a combination of factors including congestion, the propensity to save rather than consume, and a powerful work ethic. At the same time, the overwhelming majority of Japanese as well as Americans now consider themselves a part of the middle class. Self-confidence—even arrogance—has grown, moreover, as Japanese compare their successes with the recent course of others, including the United States.

Pacific Forum

Shared Views on Northeast Asia

These perceptions and conditions do much to shape the character and even the specifics of U.S. and Japanese foreign policy. It should be noted at the outset that on many political issues, and especially those relating to the Pacific-Asian region, the element of compatibility—indeed, identity—between the attitudes and policies of the two countries is dominant. The Korean peninsula is a case in point. Successive Tokyo governments have recognized that stability on the Korean peninsula and the survival of a strong South Korea are essential to the security of Japan. Despite the continuance of ethnic prejudices on both sides, a network of economic ties between Japan and ROK has been built up over the past two decades, and this is now being supplemented by a growing political interaction, even modest strategic connections. Toward North Korea, meanwhile, Japan maintains limited trade, and accepts overtly pro-North Korean activities among a portion of its Korean population. But it has also applied sanctions against Pyongyang in response to North Korean terrorism.

Both the United States and Japan would welcome cross recognition of the two Koreas and their simultaneous admission into the United Nations, steps currently vetoed by the North. Both are pleased with the recent steps toward cross contact taken by the PRC and the USSR. Both welcome the movement toward greater political openness in the South, and hope that the very timid steps toward turning out by the North will quicken together with a resumption of the North-South dialogue.

In sum, there are no significant differences between the United States and Japan with respect to the issues relating to Korea, and this was one of the first instances in which Japan played a low key political role, transmitting messages between the United States and China relating to their respective Korean policies. In recent years, policies toward the Korean peninsula have evoked a minimum of partisanship in the United States, and even in Japan, where the Socialist Party has historically maintained friendly ties only with the DPRK, there has recently been a recognition that JSP contacts with the ROK should be initiated.

Relations with the communist states other than North Korea that surround Japan in Northeast Asia are of signal importance to both Washington and Tokyo, and once again, a growing compatibility of U.S. and Japanese policies can be noted. Japan recognized the Mongolian People's Republic at an earlier point. The United States took that step more recently. However, the big issues pertain to relations with the People's Republic of China (PRC) and the USSR. The China issue is certain to loom large in Japan and the United States in the future as in the past. Put succinctly, both nations have fashioned a relationship with the PRC that is realistic, non-ideological and basically compatible with China's interests. In neither case are policies wholly pleasing to Beijing, but on balance, they are acceptable.

China's current foreign policy is fashioned around two intertwined objectives: military security and economic development. Its tactics are to combine a reduction of tension with the Soviet Union with a tilt toward Japan and the United States. That tilt has particular reference to the economic resources that China hopes to obtain from these two countries both for its industrial and military development. It thus extends beyond a simple economic relationship to encompass cultural and even security ties.

Despite the fact that a process of normalization in Sino-Soviet relations is underway, Chinese relations with Japan and the U.S. dwarf those with the USSR at present, and that is likely to continue. Geopolitical factors alone suggest that the element of mistrust in Beijing's relations with Moscow will not be easily dissipated. To this must be added the natural limits that are posed to Sino-Soviet economic interaction by virtue of the two nations' differing capacities and needs at this stage of development. There is great interest in the reform efforts being undertaken in both societies, and depending upon the course of those reforms, a greater ability to interact might evolve, but more likely it would be the accelerating effort of each to interact with the major market economies of Asia and Europe. In sum, few of the conditions exist for close relations between the PRC and the USSR, now or in the foreseeable future. It is more likely that both nations will turn to others to strengthen their position vis-a-vis one another.

For neither Japan nor the United States, however, will relations with China be smooth. Indeed, the last several years have witnessed a certain deterioration in Sino-Japanese relations, and the emergence of thorny issues between Washington and Beijing. One can never forget that the force of Sinocentrism is extraordinarily powerful in Beijing. With the decline of the Marx-Lenin-Maoism, nationalism has become an ever more vital weapon as a talented people wrestle with the disadvantages of scale and system. The grievances of Beijing's leaders with Japan can be summarized under both economic and politcal-strategic headings: Japan, concentrating upon trade and acquiring in the process sizable surpluses, became increasingly cautious with respect to investment and technology transfer. On the political front, Japanese nationalism reflective of the past enjoyed a rebirth as evidenced by the revision of textbooks, the visit of officials to Yasukuni shrine, and a new arrogance in Japanese behavior. The accelerating rearmament program accompanying these developments was thus doubly worrisome. Finally, as the Kyoto dormitory case illustrated, Tokyo still paid homage to a one-China, one-Taiwan policy despite denials. These have been the recent charges.

Japan's responses have been muted but direct: China itself bears responsibility for earlier substantial trade imbalances, with provincial authorities allowing extensive purchases of consumer goods. Abrupt changes in Chinese economic policies, together with the reluctance of the government to provide promising conditions for foreign investors, have discouraged Japanese as well as other foreign entrepreneurs. The threat of Japanese nationalism has been greatly exaggerated; Japan's military expenditures, defensive in nature, are scarcely sufficient to meet the obligations undertaken as part of the U.S.-Japan security agreement.

Behind these issues lie more fundamental considerations. China expects Japanese assistance in the present as well as subsequent stages of its economic modernization, and it is not reticent in seeking loans as well as other forms of economic support. For its part, the Japanese private sector is gearing up for a long-term extensive commitment to involvement with China. The charges of "sharp practices" and "over concentration on the Chinese market" on the one hand, and "ineptitude" on the other hand are an inevitable part of the process of rising economic interaction. But there is a concern in certain Japanese quarters about the boomerang effect of aiding China economically.

As China has reordered its domestic priorities, relegating military modernization at least temporarily to a lower status, and as tension with the Soviet Union has been reduced, Beijing has been less interested in seeing Japan become a stronger military power in the region. On the other side of the coin, most Japanese want to see China make progress slowly, so that Chinese nationalism will not spill over into the broader Asian area, along with heightened economic competition. And Tokyo is content with the de facto one-China, one-Taiwan policy that has evolved in the course of the past several decades. It has no desire to see the status quo here disrupted, especially if that were to involve violence.

The issues between the United States and China bear a broad similarity to those already discussed. While somewhat more satisfied with the U.S. balance between trade and investment, the issue of technology transfer, especially as it involves COCOM regulations, is a recurrent source of friction. Chinese access to the American market is also a concern to Beijing, although compromises have been recently effected.

With the prominent exception of Taiwan, Asia is not a source of great political contention between the U.S. and the PRC. But the de facto one-China, one-Taiwan policy of Washington rankles Beijing despite the fact that it does not choose to make this a top priority issue for the present. In connection with Taiwan, the PRC is deeply concerned that time may not be on its side. Unlike the situation in Japan, however, current U.S. policies regarding both the PRC and Taiwan have strong bipartisan support. Chinese officials are sharply critical of many American policies outside of the Pacific-Asian theater, especially those toward the so-called Third World. In turn, certain U.S. Congressmen as well as a number of private citizens have recently been very critical of China's human rights record, particularly in Tibet.

The Soviet Factor

Despite political differences, however, there is a cognizance in Beijing that the United States is a distant power in comparison with the USSR, and poses no security threat. Hence, the effort goes forward to establish and maintain a low-level security relationship with Washington —an effort made more complex recently by China's large and continuing arms sales abroad, including those to Iran. Silkworm missile sales have been halted but other military supplies continue to flow to Iran and many other countries, creating a potentially serious problem for the future.

Nevertheless, in comparison with Japan, there is probably a larger constituency in the United States for the thesis that China is a meaningful strategic counterweight to the Soviet Union and must therefore be cultivated. The fact that China insists upon being considered non-aligned is regarded as necessary rhetoric. In sum, the strategic quotient in U.S. policy toward China remains a significant element, in contradistinction to Japan's more economically oriented policies; yet there is a complementarity in the two policies that is obvious. And the United States also draws important distinctions between types of support that are important but benign and those that might boomerang.

Is there a similar compatibility between U.S. and Japanese policies toward the USSR? There is, of course, a major difference in the perspectives of the two nations. The United States must always consider the global strategic balance. In addition, it must be fully aware of the degree to which U.S.-USSR relations are played out before a global audience with the resultant politicization of those relations in Europe, Asia, and elsewhere. Japan's worldwide economic interests have thus far figured only peripherally in its relations with the Soviet Union. These relations have been governed partly by economic and political factors, but are primarily dominated by security considerations.

It is natural, therefore, that Japanese policy toward Moscow has been and will continue to be alert to trends in U.S.-Soviet relations. There is, however, an innate hostility between Japan and the Soviet Union that has deep roots in history as well as in more recent times. And that hostility is reciprocated. Hence, the psychological setting is not conducive to major improvements in bilateral Japanese-Soviet relations. On the other hand, one might presume that if Moscow were to make some significant concession, especially with respect to the northern islands, a new tone might emerge. At least equally important, the Soviet issue epitomizes a much broader question: is the Japanese private sector prepared to pursue an apolitical market foreign policy separate from, and on occasion, contrary to the government's efforts to use economic policies for political and strategic purposes? Even within the Japanese government, past divisions on this basic issue have existed, for example, between the Foreign Ministry and MITI. In any case, no issue is likely to loom larger in the immediate future. The reference here is not to clearly illegal actions such as the Toshiba case, but to trade, investment, and technology transfer that are legal but may not be in conformity with official political-security objectives. Moscow, for example, is a constant host to diverse Japanese entrepreneurs seeking to compete with their West European counterparts for opportunities not in Siberia but in the European sector of the USSR where the greatest potential for growth in the near future exists.

This contradiction is not wholly absent in the United States. The pressure from agricultural interests played a major role in causing the Reagan administration to lift the embargo against grain sales to the Soviet Union. One is reminded of Lenin's famous saying, "The capitalists will sell us the rope with which to hang them." While these are very different times from the early days of the Bolshevik Revolution, the quest of the USSR for the technology of the advanced industrial states will be unrelenting in the future as in the past, with the means used in this quest varied. Sooner or later, the nations of West Europe, the United States, and Japan must seek to define more clearly their policies with respect to this issue and the means of enforcing those policies.

This is only a portion of a much larger challenge that lies ahead. It was relatively easy for the aligned nations of the advanced world to reach agreement on how to deal with a rigid, menacing Soviet Union. Agreement on how to deal with a flexible Soviet Union will be far more complex. As the USSR seeks greater economic involvement with market economies, increased participation in conferences dealing with regions of crisis and agreements on complex disarmament measures, coordinated responses from the democratic nations will be essential. Yet even within the latter nations, differences of opinion are rife. What are Gorbachev's chances of success in his bold reform efforts? Which is better for others, a "successful" or a "failed" USSR? Such issues only touch the surface of controversies that will know no end.

The Soviet Union will "reform" in my view, whether under

Gorbachev or some successor. It will reform because it has no alternative if it is to be competitive in the 21st century. Moreover, a reforming Soviet Union, with its decision-making processes made more complicated by that process, will be a better neighbor than a Stalinist Soviet Union. Yet as has been noted, the task of defining policies toward such a nation that combine flexibility and firmness will be formidable, and on no issue is coordination between the United States and Japan more important. It is probable that while the route will be tortuous, American-Soviet relations will improve in the years ahead. Strong competition and areas of tension will exist, but the mutual stake of the two nations in a lower-cost, lower-risk foreign policy will be conducive to accommodation, even cooperation on some fronts. Indeed, since the USSR will have increasing problems of empire both within and outside its boundaries, it would not be surprising if it turned increasingly to the West for support, possibly in a dramatic manner at some point. In any case, it will always regard its "minority" populated Central Asian frontiers along with underdeveloped Siberia as potentially vulnerable. That psychology has long governed Russian attitudes toward Asia, and it is more likely to grow rather than diminish. Where this will lead Soviet policies toward the Pacific-Asian region is one of the supreme questions to be pondered.

The Opportunity of Southeast Asia

Meanwhile, the United States and Japan both recognize the significance of Southeast Asia economically and in political-strategic terms. Several critical political factors dominate this area: the growth of complexity as second or third generation elites come to power, and a quest for greater political openness emerges from the socioeconomic revolution that is ongoing; the stretching of governance as efforts to revitalize local and provincial politics are combined with regional efforts like the Association of Southeast Asian Nations (ASEAN) and an Indochina federation; continued evidence that Leninist-style socialism has grave political as well as economic deficiencies—the tragic case of Indochina, abandoned by the United States and still encased in misery; finally, the likelihood that all of the major states of the Pacific-Asian region will continue to be involved in Southeast Asia for the foreseeable future—a dramatic change from the time when only the United States had a significant presence here.

The implications of these facts for the U.S. and Japan must be under continuous study. As in other settings, Japan intends to pursue a policy that rests upon a program of economic assistance combined with a willingness to serve as "bridgehead" between Vietnam and others if the opportunity later presents itself. Ideas like "a Japanese Marshall plan" have been advanced, and various offers combining official and private sector assistance are now proffered. The response is mixed. The states comprising ASEAN want Japanese assistance—and access to Japanese markets—and they recognize that Japan is rapidly acquiring a towering economic presence in the region. Yet specific grievances with Japanese economic policies are numerous, and beyond this, Japan evokes a suspicion that is compounded out of history and cultural differences.

The United States faces fewer psychological and political barriers, although the Philippines remains a separate case, being an ex-colony. There, the U.S. is a special target of the left, and will remain a part of political disputation, irrespective of domestic trends. Elsewhere in ASEAN, the primary question about the United States can be summed up in one word—credibility. Is the U.S. sufficiently concerned and committed to pursue any given line of foreign policy—especially in this region—over time? What are the implications of the Guam Doctrine for the future? Do circumstances dictate a greater degree of self-reliance, as indicated by new trends in Australian security doctrine?

Having botched earlier opportunities, Vietnam looks at the United States with recurrent hope. Hanoi has made it patently clear that it would like U.S. recognition and assistance, both to increase its prestige and to present it with the option of playing off one force against another that it lacks today. At some point, the U.S. will establish diplomatic relations with Vietnam, but that is not likely to occur until the withdrawal of Vietnamese forces from Cambodia has taken place. Basic U.S. policy has been to follow the lead of ASEAN with respect to Indochina, and to attempt in a modest way to conciliate ASEAN and PRC policies on the issues involved. It is cognizant that all the the ASEAN states—even Thailand—view China as a potential long-term problem, and that the varying degrees of this concern have produced the current fissures in ASEAN political unity. It also appreciates the fact that sooner or later, Vietnam will have to reach some accommodation with the PRC unless it wants to live in a state of permanent militarism and dependence on an external power.

The political-strategic factors governing Southeast Asia make cooperation between the United States and Japan essential, even though the element of economic competition between them will remain strong. Japan cannot "go it alone" in this region except at its peril, given the psychological and political climate. The United States is not prepared to carry heavy burdens by itself or in disproportionate amounts. Preparations for the future in both Southeast Asia and South Asia should be underway now. The post-Cambodia and post-Afghanistan eras are likely to raise new and complex questions for the foreign policies of our two nations. Already, we can see in dim outline the possibility of changed relations between the U.S. and India, for example, despite the obstacles. Meanwhile, Japan is rapidly increasing its economic presence in this region.

An Agenda for Asia for the Future

If my focus has been upon Asia thus far, the reason is that it is this vast area that constitutes the heartland of American-Japanese interaction. In economic terms, however, the triangular relations between the U.S., Japan and West Europe has had a growing importance too great to be overlooked by any discerning observer. And while the political institutions of West Europe now seem firmly planted, the great question of the future relates to the extent to which the old Gaullist vision will be realized. That vision was of a Europe united from the Atlantic to the Urals—a Europe crossing ideological-political boundaries in the course of a socioeconomic revolution with the certain cultural-ethnic commonality in the background. Shall we witness a radically new form of regionalism in the decades ahead?

At present, Japan plays a very limited role in international politics. Witness its low posture in the United Nations. Can and should this continue? Can a nation so powerful on the economic front eschew responsibility for helping to formulate and advance political policies in the few forums available to us? As the Japanese people wrestle with the questions of Japan's role in the world, this among other questions warrants sustained attention.

If the themes examined in this essay for the past have validity, what is to be done in the future? More specifically, what step might the United States and Japan take jointly to improve their bilateral political relations and at the same time, improve the regional and global climate for peace and development? I would suggest the following actions as concrete steps.

First, at official levels, political consultation should be strengthened and regularized, being a coequal counterpart to and integrated with the various economic and defense consultations that are ongoing.

Second, a quasi-permanent, unofficial America-Japan Council should be established with the specific mandate to study all issues—economic, political, and security—that will have continuing significance to our two nations. It should be composed of key representatives from business, labor, academia, and other sectors of each society except currently active civil or military officials. Membership chosen by the two governments should be renewable for three terms of three years each, enabling continuity, with rotation after that time on a staggered basis. The Council should be empowered to hire outside experts to prepare studies.

Its findings and recommendations should be regularly submitted to the two governments. It should generally avoid the immediate crises better handled by governments. Its primary function should be to anticipate new problems or issues as well as to discern new approaches to permanent concerns.

Third, a plan of apprenticeships between the U.S. and Japan should be established, whereby individuals—generally under the age of 40—would be in residence in the opposite country for periods of one to three years, attached to appropriate universities, institutes, businesses, labor councils, or official agencies. Such individuals should be nominated by the unit from which they come, and be guaranteed the right of return to that unit. A bilateral committee would make the final selections. The costs would be borne from funds privately raised.

Fourth, Americans and Japanese should promote multilateral conferences, both quasi-official as represented by the Pacific Economic Cooperation Conference and academic in nature. The latter type of meeting is illustrated by the Quadrilateral Conferences which have been developed under the joint sponsorship of American, Japanese, Korean and ASEAN institutes. These conferences have taken under consideration the largest issues currently confronting the Pacific-Asian region, with the publication of the papers in diverse languages.

One central truth must never be forgotten. Present and future conditions guarantee that the fate of the United States and Japan will be inextricably joined. The issue, therefore, is whether we are sufficiently farsighted to make efforts now to shape that future to the benefit of our two peoples and the rest of the world.

ROBERT A. SCALAPINO
Director of the Institute of East Asian Studies, University of California at Berkeley. Robson Research Professor of Government, Professor of Political Science and Editor of Asian Survey. *Founder, First Chairman and now Board Member of the National Committee on U.S.-China Relations. He has written some 300 articles and 27 monographs on Asian politics and U.S. Asian policy. A recent book is* Major Power Relations in Northeast Asia *(1987). Member of numerous editorial boards and committees for educational and government agencies. Ph.D. Harvard University. Member of the Board of Directors, Pacific Forum.*

A Japanese Agenda for Asian Politics and Security

Seizaburo Sato

The political, economic and security framework that has defined the international system since the end of World War II is undergoing major change with important implications. There are four aspects to this— America's role, communist economic performance, reduced military tensions and cooperation in economic areas. First, there is as Professor Scalapino points out the relative decline of American military and economic superiority. At the peak of "Pax Americana", the post-World War II world revolved around the U.S. which was preeminent, outdistancing all other nations. At present, however, the Soviet Union has reached a parity with the U.S. military, and the economic rise of Japan, the European community (EC) countries and the Asian newly industrialized countries (NICs) (South Korea, Taiwan and Singapore) has faded the sheen of American greatness. In 1986, the U.S. fell into the position of the world's largest debtor nation, and in its place Japan became the world's largest creditor nation.

Second, among the communist nations, including the Soviet Union, there is a serious "crisis of performance." What is important is the fact that the leaders of communist states have become aware of the need for fundamental institutional reform if they are to have economic development.

Third, there is now a fresh effort toward the relaxation of U.S.-Soviet tensions as a prerequisite for both sides to resolve the difficult problems responsible for their waning influence and economic decline. It is still a fresh memory that the historic Reagan-Gorbachev talks of December 1987 produced an agreement on the scrapping of all ground-based INF missiles. And, even though fraught with difficulties, there will be an agreement, if only in principle, on the 50% reduction of strategic nuclear weapons. It may seem a meager beginning in arms reduction, but when viewed against the last 40 years of continuous and severe East-West confrontation, it is epoch-making.

Fourth, there is the extensive progress with the reduction of regulations and trade barriers which greatly enhances economic interdependence. Also, as a result of the recent currency exchange rate fluctuations, the Asian NICs, particularly South Korea and Taiwan, are rapidly emerging as the world's new centers of production.

The implications of these changes are far more dramatic than they might appear on the surface. First, the decline of U.S. military superiority and the Soviet Union's pursuit of military preeminence has meant an enlargement of the Soviet military threat. Despite the slump in the Soviet economy, and even with the relaxation of tensions between the U.S. and the Soviet Union, there is not yet any clear evidence that the Soviet military buildup is being harnessed, especially the buildup and modernization of naval and air forces in the Western Pacific. Nor is there any evidence indicating change in the Soviet force structure and deployment despite indications that a re-evaluation is being made by the Soviet Union of its military strategies. Still, the stagnation of the Soviet-type communist regime has seriously flawed the nation's image and weakened the Soviet Union's overall influence.

The relative decline of U.S. economic power coincided with significant global economic integration and the shift of growth centers to East Asia seriously destabilizing the international economic order. This gives rise to protectionist sentiments in the U.S. and the European community. Also, economic friction between the U.S. and EC on the one hand and Japan and the Asian NICs on the other has produced serious problems. This cycle of economic confrontation and stagnation could also compound economic problems resulting in serious damage to the bonds and solidarity of the Western Alliance.

The Asian Military Situation

Three issues are critical when one focuses on the Asia-Pacific region. First, military relations between the United States, the Soviet Union and China are now more stable. The Soviet naval and air buildup in the region is impressive. This has been accomplished mainly by turning the

Sea of Okhotsk into a Soviet submarine-launched ballistic missile (SLBM) base, adding tremendously to the strategic importance of the region. There is also direct access to Vietnam's Cam Ranh Bay naval facilities. Nevertheless, the East-West military balance still remains in the West's favor and the Soviet military threat in Asia is relatively weak compared to that of Europe and the Middle East. China's anti-Soviet and pro-Western posture became more pronounced during the 1970s and its economic and military relationships with the West grew during the 1980s as it adopted a new open-door foreign policy toward the outside world. In political and military terms, however, China has come to assume more of a neutral position in relation to the two superpowers. In this, China has achieved a certain equilibrium in its relations with both America and the Soviet Union.

Second, Asia is now and will be in the future the growth center of the world economy. Taking full advantage of the favorable conditions of a cheaper U.S. dollar, the fall of oil prices and the worldwide drop in interest rates, the Asian NICs (South Korea and Taiwan) have been hard at work consolidating their new positions as major trading nations. Within ASEAN, the Philippines fell victim to the vicious cycle of political turmoil and economic stagnation while Malaysia and Indonesia continue to suffer from low international prices for primary commodities. But the region as a whole has retained strong growth potential. For these and other reasons, the Soviet Union has made clear in Gorbachev's Vladivostok speech that it is anxious to participate in Asia's developing economic activities.

Third, even though there are conflict flash points like the Korean peninsula, Indochina and Taiwan, local strife is more easily containable than before. South Korea has clearly come out ahead with its impressive economic growth. Moreover, the peaceful process of political democratization has made significant progress since last year, diminishing the possibility to the very minimum of North Korea's making aggressive moves to take advantage of internal chaos in the South. As seen in the case of the bombing of the Korean airliner in 1987, there is still the possibility of dangerous acts of terrorism by North Korea. What North Korea can actually do remains severely limited so long as China and the Soviet Union do not support any Korean adventurism. Furthermore, trade and cultural exchanges between South Korea and China have seen rapid growth. It can be expected that similar relationships will soon develop with the Soviet Union. The deepening of these ties between South Korea on the one hand and China and the Soviet Union on the other will have a significant effect on the stabilization of the Korean peninsula. With respect to the Indochina peninsula, conditions today point to a better chance of the Vietnamese forces pulling out Cambodia. This would be because of the worsening of

Vietnam's economic crisis, the relaxation of the Sino-Soviet tensions and the favorable view toward Vietnam among the ASEAN nations. Progress in Taiwan's democratization process, its economic self-confidence, and the progress in China's open-door policy are all positive factors in further stabilizing PRC-Taiwan relations.

It goes without saying that not every change augurs for a better future. Despite the progress of the U.S.-Soviet arms control and the arms reduction talks, the Soviet military buildup in the Asian region continues unabated. The rise of protectionist sentiment and slow economic growth in the U.S. and the EC countries have cast a dark shadow over the growth prospects of the Asian NICs and the ASEAN nations. If economic friction between Japan and the U.S. is permitted to escalate as Edward Lincoln argues in this volume, the region is likely to face formidable economic difficulties in the years ahead.

Converging Japanese and American Interests

A period of major transition can be defined as a time in which traditional regimes and institutions are no longer functioning as they did and no new framework to replace it is yet in sight. By definition such periods are awash with uncertainties and perils. In order to survive in these uncharted waters without a major disaster and proceed to reconstruct a more peaceful and prosperous international order, what sort of cooperative relationship should Japan and the U.S. work out between them, and what would be a new, fairer share in the distribution of roles and responsibilities?

First of all, it ought to be emphatically stated that the increasing convergence of political and security interests of Japan and the U.S. has reached a new level in recent years and that the mutual understanding of their differing responsibilities has never been so thorough. The most important factor in the convergence of interests has been the worldwide strengthening of the Soviet military capabilities since the 1970s, especially the Soviet military presence in East Asia and the Western Pacific, with the conversion of the Sea of Okhotsk into a sea bastion for Soviet SLBMs. The joint Japan-U.S. effort of defending the Japanese archipelago from Soviet threats has overlapped with the defending of the U.S. mainland against the Soviet Union's strategic second strike capability. Also, preventing the ascendancy of the Soviet Union's military influence, especially in the Third World, is an extremely important task not only for the U.S. (charged with the responsibility of defending the entire Western world) but also Japan because of its far-flung global economic interests.

Japanese and American interests in China, following on Scalapino's points, and elsewhere in the world have also drawn closer together regarding local issues. During the Vietnam War there was a potential conflict of interests between Japan and the U.S. Also, in the 1970s, the repeated oil crises revealed differences in the policies of Japan and the U.S. Likewise, until Sino-U.S. rapprochement was accomplished and China established its policy of neutrality toward the two superpowers, there was always a possibility of Japan and the U.S. colliding on China policy. Until relatively recently, relations between Japan and South Korea were strained. Now, however, Japanese and American policies on the Korean peninsula, Indochina, the Middle East and Central America are very similar. On China policy, too, Japan and the U.S. are pursuing the same basic policies.

Despite this progress there is still room for greater cooperation. In Japan today there is a growing realization that it can no longer continue to rely upon the U.S. to defray the entire cost of maintaining international peace and prosperity, and that Japan will have to take on a greater burden. Moreover, Japan and the U.S. have come to understand more clearly that the primary security role that Japan should play is to contribute internationally through economic means. Thus, despite the continuation of economic friction, political and security cooperation between Japan and the U.S. has never been on a firmer foundation.

If and when there would ever be a military confrontation between the U.S. and the Soviet Union, it would most likely develop into a nuclear war. Because of this, the U.S. and Soviet Union have taken cautious steps to avoid such an event. Since regional conflict nevertheless remains a serious potential starting point for conflict escalation, and since such battles are likely to be in the developing world, more should be done to avoid these flash points from becoming issues. It is very possible for Japan and the U.S. to contribute toward reducing tensions in these areas if both sides can cooperate in seeking the optimum combination and application of their military, economic and political forces.

Japan and the U.S. must also work together for the consolidation of political stability in the developing nations. While political stability is a problem to be addressed by the leaders of each nation with the backing of their own people, foreign economic assistance, used carefully, can help significantly with the institution building process. While economic development does not immediately lead to political stability, it nevertheless exerts a favorable influence in the long run on the overall process of achieving it. Indeed, there are potentially hazardous cases of authoritarian leadership transition among the developing nations. But the possibility of any of these creating a revolutionary situation, as was the case in the Philippines toward the end of the Marcos administration, is extremely remote because of the tangible results of recent economic growth. In the Philippines, economic difficulties indeed produced the political chaos and weakened the country's resilience providing a fertile ground for penetration by external influences. Therefore, the issue that must be addressed by Japan and the U.S. is the reinforcing of political stability to provide appropriate economic aid and cooperation. Also, an international environment for Asia conducive to economic development must be preserved. The reconstruction of the earlier free and stable international order should not remain as a policy theme of international economic reform alone. It has obvious political and security implications as well.

The strengthening of conventional deterrence against the Soviets in the East Asia-Pacific region through Japan-U.S. cooperation is also important, not only for the security of both nations, but also for the stability of the region. Conventional deterrence provides an effective counter to a severely limited Soviet forward deployment. It also has a global purpose in that it tends to make the Soviet military behavior elsewhere in the world more cautious than otherwise, especially in Western Europe. Of course, given the Japanese Constitution, Japanese military capability must remain limited to defensive and conventional forces. Japan's acquisition of a powerful offensive capability (even a nuclear force) would not only unnecessarily provoke the Soviet Union, but it would also raise concerns among the allied nations including the U.S.—a possible element of instability to the detriment of Japan-U.S. security interests. All of this suggests a list of future priorities for Asian stability.

An Agenda for the Future

Expanded Surveillance.

To strengthen its deterrence against the Soviet Union, Japan should acquire information on the Soviet Far Eastern force movements. This will reduce the chance of a successful first attack by the Soviets. However it is not enough to rely upon the existing air, ground and sea surveillance systems, even if they are closely integrated. In addition, Japan ought to acquire surveillance systems like AWACS (Airborne Warning and Control System), OTH (over-the-horizon) radar and SURTASS (Surveillance Towed Array Sonar System) and consolidate them into a more effective surveillance system. Japan should also have its own surveillance and early warning satellites so that it can closely and continuously scan the ocean areas up to 1,000 nautical miles from its coastline. Japan also needs a real-time surveillance data exchange network with the U.S. This would include the integration of the U.S.'s Amchitka OTH radar system, which covers the entire Sea of Okhotsk area, with a Japanese system.

Extended Air Defense Capability.

If the Soviet Union started military actions in the areas adjacent to Japan, the first-stage Soviet action would be focused on Japan's land-based air force bases, radar sites and vessels operating at sea using aircraft-borne and vessel-borne missiles as well as land-based long-range missiles. To assure the effectiveness of Japan's deterrence against such a Soviet attack, the extended surveillance capability mentioned earlier must also be reinforced by a strengthened air defense capability against air attacks. Therefore, along with the BADGE (Base Air Defense Ground Environment) System being inaugurated in 1988, Japan's air defense capability should be strengthened by reinforcing the existing F-15 fighter-interceptors and the Patriot ground-to-air missiles. Also, there should be the introduction of AWACS and air tankers, the strengthening of the seaborne vessel air defense capability with the deployment of an AEGIS fleet and ATM (Anti-Tactical Missile) system which will stretch the present defense perimeter along the Japanese shoreline and cover the open ocean of the Northwestern Pacific. Indeed, if Japan's own mainland defense and the joint Japan-U.S. operations capabilities are to be really upgraded, the securing of air superiority and the guarding of the logistic supply route from the U.S. mainland are critical. The importance of an expanded air defense capability at this juncture can hardly be exaggerated.

Strengthened Anti-Submarine Warfare Capability.

The Soviet Pacific Fleet does not have a large enough aircraft carrier to provide effective air cover for a naval fleet operating in open sea. The only Soviet vessels that can operate in open sea in war, beyond the perimeter of aircover by land-based aircraft, are certain classes of attack submarines. By strengthening ASW (Anti-Submarine Warfare) capabilities against these vessels, deterrent capability against the Soviet Union itself is improved. To do this, first the existing airborne anti-submarine system must be reinforced by introducing updated versions of P-3C III and SH-60, and the SOSUS (Sound Surveillance System) network must be reinforced by introducing SURTASS. Opening an ASW center dedicated to the analyzing, evaluating and storing of sonic data as well as the research and analysis of ASW tactics is needed. Also, it is necessary to upgrade the capability to block the passage of vessels through three straits, the only open passages for the Soviet attack submarines from their home base into the Sea of Okhotsk to the ocean. Submarine attack capabilities must also be enhanced by improving upon the existing anti-submarine torpedo, aircraft, surface and sub-surface vessel capacities. Further, it is important that Japan and the U.S. develop a system to expand the exchange of information on Soviet submarines in the waters surrounding Japan. A joint system should be built to permit an effective use of information for respective ASW operations.

Strengthened Mainland Defense Capability.

Improving upon an expanded surveillance capability, an extended air defense capability and the development of ASW capability are the requisite conditions for enhancing the country's combat capabilities in an integrated war effort with the U.S. This also strengthens Japan's mainland defense capability. However, this will not suffice for a total mainland defense. In addition, the Japanese Self Defense Forces' readiness and preparedness, the survivability of its bases and the central command, and sustainability based upon better emergency stockpiling of the needed weapons and ammunitions must be accomplished. Integrated inter-service operations of the Ground, Maritime and Air Self Defense Forces must also be improved. There should be an early effort to improve the interoperability of the three branches of the armed forces and the clarification of the relationship between the Joint Staff Council and the three Self Defense Forces. In addition, there should be a review of a) the relationships between the Chairman of the Joint Staff Council and the Prime Minister who also holds the office of the Supreme Commander of the three armed forces, b) the expansion of the authority of the Joint Staff, c) the geographical redefinition and the standardization of the technical terms among the uniquely different systems of the three armed services, and d) the integrative reorganization of command and communications systems. All of this is central to an emergency preparedness strategy. In the course of integrating inter-service operations it will also be necessary to plan an integrated exercise on a national scale involving the Prime Minister, the Director General of the Defense Agency, the Maritime Agency, the National Police Agency and other related government agencies.

Wartime Host Nation Support.

Enhancing joint Japan-U.S. operations requires a wartime support operations plan where Japanese forces are standing by ready to come to the support of the U.S. combat forces. While peacetime host nation support is important, organizing the wartime support is still more important from the viewpoint of strengthening deterrence against the Soviet Union. The U.S. should negotiate a wartime host nation support agreement with attention to related documents including the 1982 U.S.-West German agreement. The terms should be that Japan will provide the U.S. forces coming to the rescue with a great variety of goods and services through the collaboration of the Self Defense Forces and the private sector organizations ranging from physical facilities, troop transport, equipment repair, supplies and provisions, installation of communications systems, telephone and teletype installation and all conceivable goods and services including procurement of a labor force. Also, since Hawaii's lightly armed 25th Infantry Division and similar units would be deployed, it is necessary for Japan to go ahead with POMCUS (Prepositioning of Overseas Material Configured to Unit Set) stockpile arrangement to provide for possible deployment in Hokkaido. Further, in order to enhance the long-term sustainability of the Japan-U.S. forces, it will be important for them to work together developing a reliable system of supply routes for additional wartime troop deployment and supply transport.

Joint Research, Development and Production of Weapons.

Technologies are generally divided into three kinds: civilian, military and dual use basic applications; the last category expanding in recent years. In high technology fields where Japan excels, this is especially obvious, and general-application technologies are moving from the civilian into the military field. For instance, Gallium Arsenide (GaAs) integrated circuits, which were commercially developed for civilian computer applications, are now used by the military for advanced weapons systems. Furthermore, the essential requisite for military technology applications, i.e., light weight, small in size and high in quality, are best met by the Japanese private sector high-tech industry which has an established reputation for excellent quality control and low-cost mass production techniques for the production of precision goods.

It was this that led to the decision in October 1987 that Japan's next-generation Fighter Support X (FSX) would be developed jointly by Japan and the U.S. as an advanced version of American F-16 fighters. According to this plan, the design phase of the project would start in 1989, and after the test flight in the summer of 1993 of the first prototype aircraft, the real production starts in 1994, with 1997 as the target year for actual field deployment. This is the first case of a joint Japan-U.S. weapons development project, and as such this Japanese-led joint weapons development project will remain the focus of attention as a possible model for many more similar joint weapons projects.

Since this Japan-U.S. joint FSX development project is the first such experience for both countries, problems will arise. A number of questions will be asked: how are the producers to share the production of the aircraft, what about American techno-nationalism, are there issues with the

Japanese system of dealing with classified information and the leakage of the Japanese technologies to third parties, etc? The relative decline of the competitive position of the U.S. high-tech industries in the world market, and in particular the decline of the U.S. electronics industry proven by the fact that the U.S. now depends on the Japanese high-tech electronic parts and components for the production of advanced weapons systems considered indispensable for national security, have been the source of American irritation in recent years. The U.S. has been adamant in insisting on maintaining its technological superiority in the weapons field in relation to Japan, other Western allies and the Soviet Union. Japan will make a careful review of the situation to decide how to best comply with the U.S. request for information secrecy as well as third party technological transfer. For Japan, working as a member of the Western camp, it must modernize its conventional forces and the effective linkage of the Japanese and the American high technologies is essential. Therefore, the FSX joint development project must be successful.

These six points for the strengthening of Asian regional security are an essential component of an agenda for the future. They are another dimension to the institutional issues raised in the earlier paper and form the foundation for the economic issues discussed later in this volume.

SEIZABURO SATO
Professor, Department of Social and International Relations, University of Tokyo. Serving as member of several Prime Ministerial Commissions including: U.S.-Japan Advisory Commission (Wisemen Group); Commission for Administrative Reform; and late Prime Minister Ohira's study group on Comprehensive Security. Served as an advisor to Prime Minister Yasuhiro Nakasone. His publications include Freedom and Integration *(1985),* The LDP Government *(1986), and* Local Government in Japan *(1986).*

The Economics of U.S.-Japan Relations in the Asia-Pacific Region

Edward Lincoln

Economics and strategic issues are not easily separated in reality. The attempt to separate them reflects a long-standing division of responsibility between economists and political scientists and the problems in this compartmentalization are nowhere more evident than in Asia. Asia is where many of the important developments over the past decade have been economic, and where the interplay of economic factors has critical importance for the evolution of strategic relations. The trends are evident: regional military conflict has diminished and rivalry among the major powers is unlikely; ideology has become less dominant with economic performance more dominant in defining national goals; and relations among nations in the region has come to depend to a large extent on how they conduct their economic relations. In this essay I will explore some of those developments, focusing on the U.S.-Japan economic relationship and the implications of these ties for the rest of the Asia-Pacific region.

Many of the ideas about the importance of U.S.-Japan relations for others in the region are not new.[1] What was evident a decade ago is even more evident and important now. In addition, major shifts are taking place within the region that go beyond the evolutionary changes of the past several decades. The movement of the United States to debtor status, of Japan to creditor status, and the dramatic rise of the yen against the dollar (and other currencies) have all been historic changes with profound implications.

Pacific Forum

From Japan's standpoint, the United States is by far its most important economic partner; it is the destination of 37% of Japan's exports (in 1985), 29% of its cumulative foreign direct investment, and several hundred billion dollars of its total overseas investment. From the U.S. perspective, Japan is its largest trading partner after Canada (taking 11% of U.S. exports in 1985), as well as the destination for a modest four percent share of U.S. overseas investment (which is more geographically diversified than Japan's). In purely economic terms, both sides have benefited enormously from this relationship despite bilateral trade problems.

Favorable Conditions After 1945

After the Second World War, bilateral relations were dominated by American strength and overwhelming size relative to Japan. The Occupation of Japan after the war had a strong liberal orientation; the goal was to foster a peaceful, democratic Japan that could reenter the world. In the economic sphere, the United States allowed Japan to establish stiff import and investment barriers out of an understanding of Japan's weakness and a sympathetic attitude toward rebuilding its economy. At that time, the strong relationship between economic and strategic questions was clearly understood: a prostrate Japan could be a breeding ground for communism, and an economically strong Japan could be an integral part of American global strategy toward the Soviet Union. These perceptions were reflected in changes in Occupation policy in 1947, with a shift toward policies to encourage Japanese economic recovery.

Assisted by the paternalistic policy stance of the United States, and driven by favorable domestic economic, political, and social conditions, the Japanese economy took off. Annual economic growth from 1950 to 1973 averaged ten percent in real terms, bringing Japan into the ranks of developed industrial economies by the 1970s. But economic success eventually brought the demise of American tolerance for Japan's heavy trade and investment barriers. Beginning in the early 1960s, international pressure mounted for Japan to adopt more open policies. The Japanese response was slow and grudging (as one might expect in a nation with heavy and entrenched protection for the previous decade), but it has now slowly moved in the direction of greater openness for more than twenty years. Overt barriers—tariffs and quotas—are now generally quite low and attention has largely shifted to less visible nontariff barriers. Despite the progress, though, I would question the view of some that Japan is today an open and free economy.

During the postwar period, Japan avoided involvement in international military/strategic questions. This was a deliberate choice on Japan's part, stemming from revulsion over the militarism of the 1930s and encouraged by the new constitution renouncing military force. Economists agree that the low level of military spending in Japan allowed resources to be redirected to commercial purposes, but there is little agreement over how much this contributed to Japan's very high economic growth.[2] On the other hand, Japan's need for international trade in order to grow, its position as a member of the capitalist West rather then the Soviet bloc, and its small, defensive military establishment have all worked to make Japan a firm ally of the United States.

New Trends

Three key developments have brought important changes in bilateral relations in the 1980s. First, Japan has caught up with the industrial nations. At current exchange rates, per capita GNP in Japan actually exceeds that of the United States.[3] This change is evident in several dimensions of the bilateral relationship. Both countries have comparative advantage in high value-added manufactured goods, a rising number of American patents are being granted to Japanese firms, and investment flows from Japan to the United States have grown dramatically.

Second, Japan has become a major net creditor and the United States a net debtor. The reasons lie in macroeconomic variables. For Japan, the slowdown in economic growth associated with economic maturity brought lower rates of investment while savings remained high. The government absorbed these excess savings from the private sector in the 1970s by running a deficit funded through bond issues, but in the 1980s the government deficit shrank and the surplus savings moved abroad, showing up statistically as a current-account surplus and net capital outflow.[4] For the United States, the Reagan administration's decision to pursue simultaneous tax cuts and dramatic increases in military spending resulted in rapidly rising government deficits in the context of a society without a large pool of excess savings. The result was a swift move to current-account deficits and capital inflow to provide necessary funding. As these global balances shifted, so too did the bilateral trade balance, deteriorating from a $10 billion U.S. deficit with Japan in 1980 to close to $60 billion in 1986 and 1987.

Third, the strong dollar that accompanied the above shifts has now been reversed. From a Japanese perspective, the yen has risen over 100 percent from 1985 to 1988. This represents an enormous currency movement in a short period of time. The strong yen/weak dollar is likely to continue indefinitely as the United States extricates itself from the fiscal and international deficits of the 1980s. This currency realignment implies a falling Japanese trade and current-account surplus as its exports appear more expensive in international markets and imports appear less expensive. At the same time, it reduces the price of foreign assets to Japanese investors.

All of these changes are of historic proportions with major implications. Catching up with the West brought to an end more than a century of determined efforts to reach this goal. Japan has never been a major creditor, unless one counts Japanese investment in colonial possessions in Asia before the war (a creditor relationship of far different dimensions than its current position). The strong yen—and its likely continuance—are also a new development; tentative moves toward a strong currency in 1971-1973 and 1977-1978 were truncated by the ensuing oil shocks.

The Asian Context

It is increasingly important to see Japan-U.S. relations in an Asian context. The region is diverse with per capita GNP ranges from the highest in the world (Japan and the United States), through a number of middle income industrializing countries (the NICs plus Malaysia), to poorer countries where per capita income is less then $1,000. Economic systems also vary from free-wheeling capitalism (Hong Kong), through "developmental" capitalism (where the state guides and shapes private-sector industry), to varying degrees of socialism and communism. Most of these countries have a greater degree of state intervention in the economic system than characterizes the United States or even Japan, and the reliance on market-set prices to provide signals to the economic system varies widely.

Despite the rather extreme diversity of economic/political systems, what makes the region exciting, and what makes economic issues important, is the relative ascendancy of economic performance at the expense of politics and ideology. To a greater extent than in other regions of the world, religious, ideological, and cultural constraints to economic development have diminished as economic performance has improved. China has dropped the disastrous emphasis on ideological purity that characterized the cultural revolution and has willingly engaged in economic interaction with the non-communist world to enhance its economic performance. South Korea and Taiwan have softened their virulent anti-communist stances and now openly engage in trade and investment with China. These and other countries have reduced the scope of inefficient domestic policies or practices (such as price controls, restrictive licensing practices, high tariffs, and others) that held back economic development.

The four NICs have been more successful at doing this than the others, but overall developments are encouraging.[5]

Economic performance has strategic implications. The interest in benefiting from international business opportunities has lessened previously sharp political divisions, represented most saliently by China's new openness to the non-communist world. The emphasis on economics means that Japan and the United States can affect strategic relationships through their economic interaction with the region—bringing improved or worsened economic growth and furthering or hindering open economic ties. Handled correctly, the entire region should develop in the context of rising interaction. Should the bilateral relationship deteriorate seriously, however, the damage to the region in the form of lower growth, less stable political regimes, and international tensions could be substantial.

Growth and the trade of Asian-Pacific developing countries are important to understand in their interaction with Japan and the United States.

Rapid Growth

Table 1 presents basic data on the recent economic performance of Asian nations. In many ways the 1980s has been a troubled decade. The average economic growth of the NICs, for example, has been below their record of the 1970s, although at least three out of the four were returning to high growth by 1986 (with Singapore the exception until a burst of growth in 1987). Among the other developing nations, growth has ranged from four to seven percent (including in India and Pakistan, presented here for comparison). Only the Philippines, with its political turmoil and extensive corruption has experienced negative growth from which it is only recently recovering.

Most forecasts see continued rapid growth. The Japanese government recently predicted a seven percent growth to the year 2000 for the NICs, with nine percent for ASEAN and seven percent for China.[6] This forecast may be overly optimistic (four to six percent is more realistic for ASEAN and China), but not by much. With first Japan and now the NICs moving onto rapid growth tracks, other Asian nations have an example to follow, and face the unenviable prospect of invidious comparison if they fail to follow it.

Dependence on Trade

The four Asian NICs all have very high dependence of foreign trade, shown in Table 2. The ratio of merchandise exports to GDP ranges from 35% in South Korea to 89% in Hong Kong and 123% in Singapore.

Pacific Forum

Thailand (21%), Indonesia (21%), and the Philippines (16%), are only somewhat lower, and even China (a large continental nation that would be expected to have a low exposure to trade) has quickly emerged from near autarky to reach ten percent.

Table 1

Economic Growth in Asia

COUNTRY	1980-86 %	1986 %	GDP PER CAPITA 1986 $
U.S.	2.6	3.6	17,361
Japan	3.7	2.5	16,155
NICs			
South Korea	8.3	11.9	2,361
Taiwan	7.2	10.8	3,995
Hong Kong	1.5	8.7	6,768
Singapore	5.3	1.9	6,698
OTHERS			
China	—	—	310
Malaysia	4.4	1.0	1,725
India*	5.5	6.3	262
Pakistan	6.7	7.5	327
Thailand	4.7	3.5	801
Indonesia*	4.5	3.2	451
Philippines	- 0.6	0.2	556

*Through 1985 rather than 1986.
SOURCES: IMF, *International Financial Statistics.*

For the NICs, these high proportions have been the result of export-oriented growth strategies in the context of small (in terms of population) nations. While successful, the consequence is that the NICs, and to a lesser degree, the other nations in the region, are very sensitive to international developments. They need growth in the rest of the world plus a healthy, open trading system in order to continue their own economic growth. Only when the focus shifts from Pacific Asia to South Asia can one find nations still relatively insulated from international trade.

Japan and America in the Pacific

The real impact of the United States and Japan on the region is quite straightforward. Table 2 shows the share of each country's exports going to Japan and the United States as well as the share of their imports originating from these two. For the four NICs, the share of exports destined for the United States is extraordinarily high—from 21% for Singapore to 48% for Taiwan. Combined with the high share of exports in GDP, this means that close to one-quarter of Taiwan's economic output goes to the United States. The same is true of Hong Kong and Singapore, while a slightly lower 12% of South Korean output is destined for the United States. For all four of these countries, the United States is the dominant destination for exports, but Japan is the dominant source of imports. For the other nations in the region the percentages are generally lower, but the United States and Japan are the largest single trading partners for most. Only for the raw material producers (China, Malaysia, and Indonesia) is Japan a larger export market than the United States, and only in the Philippines is the United States clearly the larger source of imports.

Table 2

Merchandise Trade

COUNTRY	EXPORTS/ GDP %	SHARE OF EXPORTS TO: Japan %	SHARE OF EXPORTS TO: U.S. %	SHARE OF IMPORTS FROM: Japan %	SHARE OF IMPORTS FROM: U.S. %
U.S.	5	11	—	20	—
Japan	13	—	37	—	20
NICs					
S. Korea	35	15	36	25	21
Taiwan	56	11	48	28	24
Hong Kong	89	3	44	23	9
Singapore	123	9	21	17	15
OTHERS					
China	10	22	9	36	12
Malaysia	7	25	13	23	15
India	4	11	23	10	10
Pakistan	10	11	10	13	14
Thailand	21	13	20	26	11
Indonesia	21	49	23	24	18
Philippines	16	19	36	14	25

NOTES:
1. The ratio of exports to GDP for Hong Kong and Singapore include re-exports. However, for Hong Kong, the shares of trade with Japan and the United States do not include re-exports.
2. The ratio of exports to economic output in China uses national income rather than GDP.
SOURCES: IMF, *International Financial Statistics, and Direction of Trade; Taiwan Statistical Data Book;* and *Hong Kong 1987.*

Investment presents essentially the same picture. Both Japan and the United States are important investors and in most cases are the largest investors by a wide margin. In a relative sense the region is more important to Japan, with 27% of its cumulative foreign direct investment in the region, than to the United States, with only six percent. (Comparing the position of Japan to the United States in individual countries is difficult because there is no consistent international standard for measuring these amounts.) However, South Korean data shows 47% of cumulative inward direct investment from Japan and 31% from the United States, totaling an overwhelming 78%. In Taiwan 22% comes from Japan and 31% from the United States, making 53% together.[7]

One of the interesting features of Asia, in fact, is that Japan does not dominate despite its close geographical position and the cultural advantages it ought to have over the United States. This may be a deliberate choice by Asian countries. Most of them are pursuing nationalistic development strategies in which they desire to avoid excessive dependence on any single foreign power. They recognize the necessity of heavy trade and investment ties with both Japan and the United States, but prefer to play them off against each other to prevent either from becoming too dominant. The position of Japan and the United States together also implies that trade and investment ties among the other countries of the region are quite thin.

Because of this the bilateral U.S.-Japan relationship is very important to the region. Slow growth or recession in either or both has large negative consequences for others in the region. Movements of exchange rates up or down in response to macroeconomic developments either increase or reduce the incentive for American or Japanese firms to invest in factories in the region. At the moment, the forces that have brought about the rapid appreciation of the yen are bringing a wave of Japanese investments and a rise in exports to Japan. Because the other nations in the region are small, they tend to rely upon the United States to take the lead in pressing Japan to open its markets. In the reverse direction, these countries frequently fear that U.S. anger with Japan will lead to protectionist pressures against them as well. They make a point of telling Americans that they should not be placed in the same category as Japan, that Japan is the principal problem for the United States, and that they should continue to be the beneficiaries of American tolerance and indulgence. In a broader sense, serious disruptions in U.S.-Japan relations poison the atmosphere for other discussions, heightening American suspicion and reducing American tolerance of similar trade practices in other countries. Since many of the other Asian countries are following nationalistic development strategies, they, too, have substantial trade and investment barriers.

A Reluctant Japan

The fundamental problem with Japan from an American standpoint is not the large global or bilateral Japanese trade surplus *per se*, it is the strong impression that Japan remains a reluctant participant in the international economic system. To be sure, Japan has made much progress over the past two decades in opening its markets; any comparison of earlier trade and investment barriers will show Japan to be a much more accessible country today. Nevertheless, overwhelming evidence attests to the continued existence of serious and rather pervasive trade barriers.

There has been some controversy among American economists over the importance or distinctiveness of Japanese barriers, with some seeing Japan's trade patterns as fairly normal given its geographical location and other economic variables.[8] However, it is difficult to explain away the kind of differences presented in Table 3.

Table 3

Intraindustry Trade Levels

	U.S.	GLOBAL IIT INDEX JAPAN	WG	FRANCE	US/J	U.S.BILATERAL IIT LEVEL US/F	US/WG
1970	53.1	26.5	53.5	67.1	24.2	34.1	36.2
1975	57.4	18.6	51.6	64.6	23.4	40.1	38.8
1980	56.8	19.0	57.4	66.5	22.0	47.4	38.1
1985	53.6	23.4	62.8	73.8	18.3	48.6	34.8

NOTES:
1. The IIT index varies between zero (no intraindustry trade—either exports or imports equal zero) and 100 (complete intraindustry trade—exports equal imports in size).
2. Index values are adjusted for global merchandise balances using the Grubel-Lloyd technique.
SOURCE: Calculated from 3-digit industry data taken from the United Nations trade data tapes.

One of the major developments in world trade in the postwar period has been emergence of high levels of intraindustry trade: imports and exports of products identified in international industry classifications as belonging to similar industries. Japan has not shared in this important development; it tends to either export or import but not both. On a global basis, the distinctiveness of Japan is very evident. Compared to an intraindustry trade index (which varies from zero to 100) of 50 to 70 for the United States, France and West Germany, Japan has been at less than half that level, and was at a lower level in 1985 than in 1970, despite years of supposedly lowering barriers to imports that should have led to increased intraindustry trade. The United States has intraindustry trade levels with France and West Germany that are twice as high as with Japan, and they have been steady or rising while levels with Japan have been falling.

Some have tried to estimate the dollar impact of Japan's trade barriers on American exports to Japan. These estimates are not particularly high, with one recent attempt putting the amount of additional exports that the United States might generate at only $5 to $8 billion (added to existing exports of close to $30 billion).[9] But the dollar amount of the trade that is obstructed by Japanese import barriers is not as important as what Japanese behavior patterns have done to create an image of a protectionist, selfish participant in the international trading system. Despite Japan's position as a leading industrial nation with a large trade surplus, it has not become a leader (by example) within the international trade system.

Japanese officials have frequently denied the importance of trade barriers, which is part of the problem. In the United States and Europe, most protectionist barriers are obvious, but in Japan they are often hidden and deniable, but real nonetheless. The Japanese argument that foreign firms do not try hard enough to penetrate the Japanese market applies in some cases, but cannot be applied across the board as an explanation.[10] Arguments about the closeness of buyer-seller relationships in Japan, or the demands for high quality by consumers also have some truth to them, but the same can be said of other countries where American products nevertheless compete well against Japanese goods.

Japan must live with its own historical past, but there are limits to how far out of line a nation may be with general world trends without incurring the wrath of its trading partners. No matter what the domestic justification or problems, Japan cannot remain apart without jeopardizing the liberal trading system.

The United States has its problems as well. Its protectionism may be more obvious or transparent, but that is small comfort. Much of this protectionism is couched in terms of retaliation against a variety of "unfair" foreign actions (dumping, intellectual property right infringements, or just sudden surges in imports), and many of the protectionist outcomes are in the form of "voluntary" export restraints by other nations, but the implications are the same. The lengths to which the United States resorts to hide the protectionist nature of its policies can be quite absurd. The bilateral semiconductor pact of 1986 called for higher prices on Japanese-made memory chips, but then the United States Trade Representative

(USTR) complained when the response by Japan's Ministry of International Trade and Industry (MITI) was to coordinate production restrictions by Japanese manufacturers. This was an elementary matter of supply and demand; in order for the price to rise, supply had to be restricted and the government had to sanction such cartel-like behavior. Earlier comments by the administration that the voluntary automobile restraints by Japan were "better" in some sense than quotas imposed by the United States were equally absurd. The outcome was identical and the only difference was semantics. Unlike Japan, the United States also has had a strong ideological commitment to the concept of free trade.

Tempering the evidence of protectionist decisions by the U.S. government is the fact that imports rose rapidly in the first half of the 1980s. Table 4 compares the growth of American and Japanese imports from Asian countries.

Table 4

**Growth of U.S. and Japanese Imports
1980-1985**

	ANNUAL GROWTH OF IMPORTS	
FROM:	U.S. %	JAPAN %
NICs		
S. Korea	19	6
Taiwan	19	8
Hong Kong	12	6
Singapore	17	1
OTHERS		
China	29	8
Malaysia	-2	4
India	15	3
Pakistan	16	13
Thailand	12	-2
Indonesia	-2	-5
Philippines	4	-9

Sources: IMF, *Direction of Trade*.

From the four NICs, American imports rose at annual rates ranging upward from 12-19%, while Japanese imports from these countries rose at annual rates of only one to eight percent. The pattern for other Asian countries is not quite so uniform, but American imports rose faster than those of

Japan from all except Malaysia. The differences in performance are especially striking in the cases of China, India, and Thailand. Thus, despite the fact that the Reagan administration has presided over more protectionist actions than its predecessors, those actions could have had little overall impact on American imports from Asia; their growth has been high, much higher than that of Japan.[11]

Looking Ahead

The past eight years have been particularly difficult, although the two nations remain far from a trade war or a break of major proportions. The Reagan administration began with a tough position on opening Japanese markets to imports, but complicating and frustrating that push was the very strong value of the dollar during the first half of the 1980s which worked against U.S. exports. During those years, the administration pressed for action on long lists of complaints, and Japan responded with broad collections of market-opening measures, many of which were vague or did not resolve the basic problems.

In 1985, the focus moved to dealing in depth with a narrower range of issues in what was known as the market-oriented sector-specific (MOSS) approach. In the first round, negotiations dealt with telecommunications equipment and pharmaceuticals, medical equipment, forest products, and electronic products. A second round in 1986 concentrated on automobile parts. Officials involved believe that this concentrated approach was useful, but that it has left negotiators physically and mentally exhausted. Any new round of MOSS talks is unlikely in 1988 because of the impending U.S. elections and the termination of the Reagan administration.

Only two major issues were on the table at the beginning of 1988—access to construction contracts in Japan and agricultural trade—and both of these were resolved in June. But this should be interpreted as a brief lull rather than a major improvement or solution to bilateral problems. Once the U.S. presidential election is over and a new administration comes into office, a new round of complaints, negotiations, and accusations will begin. The next administration may be more willing to use retaliation against Japan as both a calculated bargaining tactic and as an expression of frustration if Japanese import behavior does not change or if negotiations do not bring progress.

The rise in the value of the yen and Japan's move to creditor status introduces new elements to the bilateral relationship. The above discussion emphasized the lack of a liberal trade lobby in Japan, but that may now change because of the strong value of the yen. Even in Japan there is a limit to tolerance of high domestic prices (relative to international prices), and that limit appears to have been reached. Manufacturers are turning increasingly to foreign sources of supply for parts, and some are expanding OEM contracts with foreign firms for finished products. Commitments to domestic firms may put limits on this process of change, but they will not block it. This increased interest in imports puts Japanese manufacturers in the position of dealing with domestic trade barriers themselves rather than having foreigners supply the pressure for change. In short, the high yen implies the beginnings of a free trade lobby in Japan that could lead to a more positive opening of markets.[12]

A second development is Japan's move to creditor status. The past several years have brought a wave of Japanese investment in the United States. In purely economic terms, this investment has brought an infusion of money, as well as technology flow and job creation in the case of Japanese manufacturing plants. But the rapidly growing size of this investment combined with the great visibility of some Japanese acquisitions may bring resentment and efforts to place controls on its continuation. To date, Japanese investment has been relatively free of criticism (with the exception of complaints from the automobile parts manufacturers, and complaints about Japanese financial institutions obtaining primary dealerships in U.S. government securities). Each nation, though, has some threshold beyond which foreign investment infringes on the sense of national sovereignty. Only a tiny portion of total American assets is held by the Japanese, but that portion may be reaching the point where national sensibilities are aroused. Japanese investors must be prepared to live with this reaction. Belief in open investment by foreigners is a concept that is even more deeply entrenched in the United States than free trade, so any serious limit to further acquisitions is remote, although the noise level could be high.

Even without complaints or efforts to limit investment, some now see Japanese (and other foreign) investment as placing constraints on American policy. The need to remedy the large current-account deficit implies that domestic economic policy goals must be sacrificed for international goals—a necessity faced by (and disliked by) other debtors around the world. Investors on Wall Street now express other concerns, wondering what the reaction will be in Tokyo to particular American economic policy decisions. Because they have become significant players in American financial markets, investors in Tokyo can exercise their voice through their actions in those markets. The size of their role and the importance of their voice may be exaggerated, but the perception that they count is now clear.[13]

Pacific Forum

Crisis Scenarios

What happens if Japan and the United States do not adjust to new realities? How difficult might the relationship become and what would happen to other Asia-Pacific nations? The very fact that such scenarios are worth outlining is a depressing development; until recently the possibility of any serious deterioration in bilateral relations appeared to be so remote that engaging in such speculation was generally dismissed as foolish. Nevertheless, let me suggest three crisis scenarios: (1) a protectionist drift, (2) a resource crisis, and (3) a diplomatic/military crisis.

Protectionist Drift

Trade problems intensify as neither the United States nor Japan alter their basic trade patterns. Younger politicians and bureaucrats in Japan drop the deference toward the United States that characterized their elders' attitudes and inflame relations by their antagonistic and arrogant behavior. American politicians and bureaucrats become increasingly disenchanted with Japan as problems continue and more frequently resort to protectionist punishments when they perceive that Japan has transgressed "fair" trade rules as defined and interpreted unilaterally by the United States.

A Resource Crisis

This could be a replay of the problems of the early 1970s. With the advent of a sudden shortage of an important resource (oil, iron ore, uranium, food, etc.), Japan perceives that the United States has treated it poorly. Indeed, it could possibly be the United States that precipitates the problem by refusing to supply Japan with a resource, as happened very briefly (and without any material damage to Japan) with soybeans in 1973. Alternatively, Japanese business and government could perceive that the United States is adopting a competitive and antagonistic stance toward Japan in dealing with a world shortage, rather than cooperating to share the burden (which was a strong fear in Japan in the wake of the first oil crisis). Feeling isolated or besieged by the United States, Japan exercises economic levers in retaliation.

A Diplomatic/Military Crisis

This scenario begins with basically non-economic events which then spill over into all aspects of the bilateral relationship. A revolution in a third world country, accompanied by the taking of U.S. hostages or U.S. deaths (civilian or military) could precipitate problems if Japan decided that its own national interest lay in preserving good relations with the revolutionary regime. This has happened in the past (the 1973 oil crisis, the 1979

Iranian revolution, and South Africa). American anger over Japan's commercially dominated foreign policy could potentially lead to economic sanctions and Japan retaliates.

Are any of these three scenarios likely? Perhaps not, but they are all plausible. The possibility that politicians or bureaucrats on either or both sides could let their anger over a particular problem overcome their rational evaluation of overall benefit is real. Japan and the United States may be close allies, but given different natural resource bases, different cultures, different histories, and different geographic settings, these two countries do not share the same perceptions of national interest. It is a mistake to assume that the United States and Japan are always motivated by common values or goals in world affairs, and those differences could burst forth at some point in a crisis situation.

Overcoming Crises

What can be done to moderate such a crisis mentality? There are several options:

The United States must get its fiscal house in order.

This should be seen as the single most important issue confronting the United States. American fiscal policy must be recognized as a central element of American foreign policy. The enormous rise in the fiscal deficit in the first half of the 1980s was a major foreign policy failure, severely damaging broad American economic/political/military objectives. Emphasizing fiscal adjustment by the United States is a more realistic policy goal than pressing for broad international macroeconomic policy coordination.

The United States must avoid a protectionist drift.

Over the next decade, the United States will need an open international trading system to absorb the coming increase in American exports as the fiscal adjustment takes place. Protectionism at home lessens the interest of others in keeping the system open; the United States must remain a leader by example. In a broader sense, the basic rationale for free trade remains unaltered. It is a sound concept that has withstood intellectual challenges from some economists and businessmen. No one expects that truly free trade will ever characterize all products or all nations, but the movement in that general direction should be maintained.

Japan must respond positively to the high yen.

The strong yen should be used as a trigger to develop a true interest in the liberal trade system. Prices are a far more effective method of generating this interest than any amount of moral suasion by prime ministers making shopping trips to department stores to buy foreign products. If Japan continues to show rapid import increases in response to the strong yen and demonstrates real movement on import barriers, it will do much to strengthen the commitment of other nations to the liberal international trading system.

The Asia-Pacific region should move toward a more open economic system.

Developing nations in the region resent being pushed in this direction, but their protectionist policies should not be allowed to prevail. These nations need to move beyond their conviction that they are the victims of the U.S.-Japan friction (with their metaphor of small animals trampled by battling elephants). Moving the successful NICs out of GSP status has been highly appropriate and a similar change should be made for other countries when they reach appropriate levels of development. As a means to encourage openness, membership in the OECD should be used as a reward. At the present time Hong Kong and Singapore are clearly at income levels that justify inclusion in the OECD, and both Taiwan and South Korea should be at those levels in a few years.

A regional organization for the Pacific should not be encouraged.

Proposals for a new organization along the lines of the OECD to bring together Pacific Basin nations have been made for more than a decade. One of those proposals (the Organization for Pacific Trade and Development—OPTAD) attracted some interest from the U.S., Australian, and Japanese governments in 1978-1979, but never materialized.[14] The smaller nations in the region seem to fear dominance by Japan and the United States. Questions of membership have also been a problem. Even though China is now integrated into many multilateral organizations, the problem of having to pick either China or Taiwan remains a thorny issue, and any realistic regional organization should have both of them. The Soviet Union is increasingly important in the region, but its intentions remain suspect to others, and the nations it supports in the region (Vietnam and North Korea) are virtually the only ones that do not participate in any meaningful or positive sense with others. A more productive route is to pull nations within the region into the OECD as they reach appropriate income levels. Participation in the OECD by Taiwan and Hong Kong, for example, could do much to clarify their future existence as independent or quasi-independent states.[15] Participation would also eliminate the very irritating lack of statistical data on these two in major international sources.[16] If this

Edward Lincoln

policy is to materialize, it must be the United States and Japan that press for admission of other Asian nations.

Special bilateral or regional free trade zones should not be encouraged.

Japan proposed a Pacific free trade area 20 years ago, but the proposal has never been favorably received. It would raise as many doubts now among developing nations in the region of Japanese and American dominance as it did then. Furthermore, the bilateral free trade zone between Canada and the United States does not represent a model for similar relationships between the United States and Asian countries. The U.S.-Canada relationship is a special one, with a common language, a long common land border, similar levels of economic development, and a great disparity in population so that Canadian industry can be efficient only when at a scale to serve the U.S. market as well. Despite recent talk, similar arrangements with Japan or Taiwan involve far fewer common interests. The U.S.-Japan (and U.S.-Taiwan) trade imbalances are large, there is no land border, and many of the true barriers in Japan are outside what could be swept away through a treaty.

These proposals would further the goal of continued economic growth and prosperity around the region. Doing so has favorable strategic implications for the United States: the danger of revolution will continue to recede and friendly contact among the nations of the region will continue to increase. We must recognize the existence of such links between economic policies and broader U.S. national interest or foreign policies.

EDWARD LINCOLN
Senior Fellow in the Foreign Policy Studies Program at The Brookings Institution. He recently completed a study of macroeconomic changes in Japan published by The Brookings Institution 1987 under the title Japan: Facing Economic Maturity *(1987). He also teaches at the Johns Hopkins University School of Advanced International Studies (SAIS). Dr. Lincoln took his A.B. in economics from Amherst College in 1971, M.A. in East Asian Studies at Yale University in 1974 and Ph.D. degree in Economics at Yale University in 1978.*

Endnotes

1. Peter Drysdale and Hugh Patrick, "Evaluation of a Proposed Asian-Pacific Regional Economic Organization," in Congressional Research Service, *An Asian-Pacific Regional Economic Organization: An Exploratory Concept Paper* (Washington: Committee on Foreign Relations, United States Senate, July 1979, committee print 46-192), discuss in some detail the emerging importance of the Asia-Pacific region and the primacy of economic issues.
2. Japan's "free ride" on defense has been a favorite point of businessmen, but Hugh Patrick and Henry Rosovsky argued in *Asia's New Giant* (Washington: The Brookings Institution, 1975, p. 45) that low defense spending is not the dominant reason for Japan's economic success and that even if defense spending had been as high as six to seven percent of GDP (i.e. roughly at U.S. levels), average annual economic growth in the 1950s and 1960s would have been lowered by only one to two percentage points.
3. Table 1 shows per capita GNP higher in the United States, but exchange rates have moved considerably since 1986, raising the dollar value of Japan's GNP.
4. The evolution of macroeconomic conditions in Japan is explored in detail in Edward J. Lincoln, *Japan: Facing Economic Maturity* (Washington: The Brookings Institution, 1988). The rise of government deficits in the 1970s was less of an intentional Keynesian response to Japan's position than an accidental result of unexpected shortfalls in tax collections as economic growth dropped below official forecasts.
5. Not all observers are as sanguine about the dominance of economics. Writing about the NICs, Lucian Pye comments, "Political legitimacy in East Asia has become inordinately dependent upon continual national economic progress. The criterion of legitimacy, to a dangerous degree, has become success in advancing economic development." (Lucian Pye, "The New Asian Capitalism: A Political Portrait," in Michael Berger and Hsin-Huang Hsiao, *In Search of an East Asian Development Model*, Transaction Books, 1988, p. 85.) If this is a problem, it is quite a welcome one compared to the extreme difficulty nations in the Mideast have had dealing with the social consequences of economic development in the context of Islamic religious traditions that have reacted negatively (and violently) to modernization.
6. Council for Economic Research on the Pacific Region for the 21st Century, *Prospects for the Pacific Age: Economic Development and*

Policy Issues of the Pacific Region to the Year 2000, Summary (Tokyo: Economic Planning Agency, July 1985, p. 10).

7. Further discussion of regional investment is contained in Edward J. Lincoln, *Japan's Economic Role in Northeast Asia* (New York: The Asia Society, 1987, pp. 25-27). The U.S. share in Taiwan may be higher than 31% because the data list overseas Chinese as a separate source of inward investment, many of whom may reside in the United States.
8. In this group are Gary Saxonhouse ("The Micro- and Macroeconomics of Foreign Sales to Japan," in *Trade Policy in the 1980s*, William Cline, ed., Washington: Institute for International Economics) plus C. Fred Bergsten and William Cline (*The United States-Japan Economic Problem*, Washington: Institute for International Economics, 1985). Recent work by Bela Belassa (manuscript in progress) and Robert Lawrence ("Closed Markets or Minds", *Brookings Papers*) have challenged this view rather convincingly.
9. Bergsten and Cline, *Ibid.*, pp. 109-114.
10. Similar explanations were recently put forth in a *New York Times* article on why prices of foreign products remain so high, and so much higher than in the United States. In some instances it may be true that American firms have deliberately chosen to keep yen-dominated prices the same despite the declining dollar, but this fails to explain the very widespread existence of large price differentials between Japan and the United States. If Japanese industry seriously wanted to import and sell foreign products at prices close to those in the United States, it could do so.
11. In 1986 and 1987, Japan's imports from the Asian NICs rose quite rapidly—although in some cases Japan's exports to these countries rose even faster, so that imbalances increased rather then fell. Despite this recent change for Japan, the point remains that Asian accusations about rising protectionism in the United States are exaggerated.
12. The rapid rise in Japan's imports from the Asian NICs in 1986 (25%) and 1987 (44%) is an encouraging sign—if it continues for several more years. If sustained, this development should be seen as the result of both an economic response to the higher yen and a shift in attitudes toward acceptance of manufactured imports from developing countries. However, at the same time that Japan's imports from these countries have risen rapidly, exports to them have risen even more rapidly so that the trade balance with the NICs remained virtually identical—$14.4 billion in 1985 and $14.5 billion in 1987.
13. Reinforcing this perception, the head of the presidential commission

investigating the October 19th stock market crash recently stated that he believed that Japanese investors precipitated the crash.
14. Hugh Patrick and Peter Drysdale, *Ibid*.
15. These are thorny questions and inclusion of these two states in the OECD would entail bending the rules. However, this option deserves serious consideration as a means of influencing Chinese behavior as Hong Kong reverts to its ownership and if any future moves toward creating a similar arrangement for Taiwan materialize.
16. Prior to China's opening to the West, the IMF published data on Taiwan in its statistical publications, and included trade data on China assembled from the data of IMF member nations. Since the ouster of Taiwan and arrival of China, though, Taiwan has completely disappeared from IMF sources. Hong Kong, because it is not a nation, is included in IMF trade data, but not in the *International Financial Statistics*. But these two are among the most important economic entities in Asia.

Reorienting the Japanese Economy for the Future

Yutaka Kosai

Since Edward Lincoln's paper was focused on economic trends up to the last couple of years, I thought it appropriate to restrict my comments to recent events, largely events in which I have played a major role. These recent events also have significant implications for the 1990s.

The "restructuring of the economy" is a phrase which has become very popular in Japan since the formation of the now well-known Maekawa Commission set up by the former prime minister, Yasuhiro Nakasone, in the fall of 1985. As a member of that Commission, I remember vividly its first meeting in a dark room at the Prime Minister's official residence. A sense of crisis prevailed at the meeting. The atmosphere was quiet and ominous. Another member who happened to sit beside me whispered, "We are playing the role of Tairo Ii, the man who promised the opening of Japan to Western powers immediately before the Meiji Restoration in face of the strong opposition at home." Ii was later assassinated by ultra-nationalistic samurai. We hope to avoid such a fate.

The fall of 1985 was a time of high tension in Japan-U.S. economic relations. The imbalances in the current account between Japan and the U.S. were mounting. The U.S. Congress was preoccupied with a number of protectionist policies. Theodore White had just written a jingoistic article in *The New York Times Magazine*. And Prime Minister Nakasone was trying to make the Tokyo Summit of May 1986 a successful political show of Japanese cooperation. Two years have now passed since the Maekawa

Pacific Forum

Report was first issued in April 1986. A year has passed since the publication of the second Maekawa Report in April 1987, and fortunately, no member of the Commission has been assassinated for what the report recommended. Instead there has been considerable progress in all areas.

The Maekawa Report took the correction of the international payment imbalances as the policy goal for Japan. To attain the goal, the report stipulated (1) the expansion of domestic demand, (2) changes in imports and the industrial structure, and (3) maintaining an appropriate level for the yen/dollar exchange rate. The importance of making positive contributions to world economic growth was also stressed as a mission for Japan.

To be sure there have been critics of the Maekawa Report. Was Japan to blame for its current surplus and not the U.S. for its deficit? Should the current surplus in the international balance of payments be narrowed when the world is seriously in need of a supply of savings? Were the measures enumerated in the report consistent with its aims? I will not go into great detail on these issues, but rather turn to the actual performance of the Japanese economy over the past two or three years and indications of new trends.

Japanese performance has subsequently exceeded the expectations of the members of the Maekawa Commission in several critical areas. First, the yen has appreciated dramatically. In the fall of 1985, when the Plaza Agreement was signed by finance ministers and central bankers of five industrial countries, a dollar was around the level of 240 yen. With the yen/dollar exchange rate half of that now, there have been dramatic changes in the import structure, industrial organization, and the balance of international payments.

Changes in the import structure have been most remarkable. In the past Japan was known as a resource importing and manufactured goods exporting country. In 1975, 80% of the imports in value terms consisted of food, energy and raw materials. In 1987, the import of manufactured goods accounted for 45% of total value of imports. The ratio is expected to continue to rise and to exceed 50% in the near future. Income elasticities for imports differ with the category of goods. According to a study by the Ministry of International Trade and Industry (MITI), imports expand by 0.2% for energy, 0.3% for raw materials and 1.6% for manufactured goods when income grows by one percent. An increased share of manufactured goods in imports implies that the average income elasticity of imports is now greater than it used to be. What was considered a structural element in the persistent current surplus of Japan has been removed.

This increase in the import of manufactured goods reflects the progress of Asian newly industrialized countries (NICs). Refrigerators, pocket calculators, videos, cameras, etc., are now flowing into the Japanese market from these countries and other regions. The strengthened Japanese appetite for a higher standard of living is also reflected in the surge of purchases of BMWs and other European cars. Ford and Japanese car makers in the U.S. are also trying to follow the European rivals by exporting to Japan. Horizontal instead of vertical, intraindustry rather than interindustry divisions of labor are emerging in Japan.

The industrial structure has responded to these changes. Industries hardest hit were largely dependent upon domestic resources. The aluminum industry, dependent upon local electricity, has virtually disappeared from Japan. The coal industry is on the verge of collapse. Labor intensive industries have also lost their comparative advantage. The dominant position of the Japanese shipbuilding industry has been replaced by Korean shipbuilders. Even iron and steel makers had to modernize in the face of severe international competition.

Increased imports, as well as progress in industrial adjustment, may cause an unemployment problem. When the unemployment ratio reached three percent in the spring of 1987, the advent of massive unemployment was seriously feared. However, the situation in the job market improved significantly with the pick-up of domestic demand. Real GNP grew by an annual rate of 7-8% in the latter half of 1987, in spite of the faltering exports and rapidly increasing imports. More than 1.7 million housing starts were reported in fiscal 1987, a figure exceeding that of the U.S. with twice the population. Personal consumption also soared, and business investment began to increase. This has continued in 1988 and will likely remain important well into the future.

Why has this explosion of domestic demand occurred? Neoclassical economists emphasize the effect of the improved terms of trade due to yen appreciation. Monetarists point to the rapid growth of the money supply, associated with an historically low level of interest rates and inflating asset values. Keynesians are satisfied with the effect of active fiscal measures taken in the fall of 1986 and in the spring of 1987. In fact, all of these factors have worked together to expand domestic demand. The ideas of the Maekawa Report have, in essence, been realized, at least in my interpretation.

The Next Phase

But is this enough? The Maekawa Report stressed the importance of rectifying the international balance of payments disequilibrium. Judging from this self-imposed standard, one can ask if the results achieved have been satisfactory. The answer is a qualified yes. The ratio of the current surplus to GNP declined from 4.7% (Oct-Dec 1986) to 3.1% (Oct-Dec 1987). Few expected such a substantial improvement within one year. However, the present level of the surplus is huge, particularly in dollar terms. An optimistic group expects the continuing improvement with the yen definitely overvalued and with a "boomerang" effect on direct investment overseas. Pessimists are afraid of the increasing surplus of investment income from accumulated assets abroad.

A recent study by a subcommittee of the Economic Council in Japan forecasts the ratio of current surplus to GNP in 1992 to less than two percent. Assuming appropriate nominal growth and an exchange rate of around 100 yen to the dollar, the size of the nominal surplus in 1992 in dollar terms will remain almost the same as 1988.

A somewhat similar development is taking place in the United States. Now U.S. exports are rising. An expansion of exports stimulates manufacturing (instead of the service sector) as well as equipment investment (instead of private consumption). The restructuring of the U.S. economy is now under way. Still, problems remain as to whether U.S. imports are to be reduced quickly enough. Since U.S. imports are almost twice the size of exports, exports have to expand twice as fast for the trade deficit to be held steady. This may not be possible. The U.S. is a large country and the small country hypothesis does not hold; when the U.S. reduces its imports, its exports cannot be expanded if the world goes into a recession as a result of the U.S. reduction of imports. Although there are some signs of improvement, the size of the remaining imbalances is still large. As a result, risks of financial instability and of a spread of protectionism cannot be dismissed for some time to come.

There are three key tasks for the future the two nations face that deserve greater discussion:

The Steady Expansion of Domestic Demand in Japan

Until recently, consumption demand appeared saturated. Automobiles, TV sets, and other consumer durables were widespread. The price of land is prohibitively high, blocking the building of new houses. Theoretically, there is no way to promote domestic demand. However, the resurgence in consumption expenditures and in housing construction since mid-1987 clearly shows the theory is wrong.

There are social issues to be corrected in this regard—the excessive concentration of economic activity in Tokyo is one such problem. The role of fiscal policy must also be redefined. A central issue is how to control bond issues. The ratio of government bonds outstanding to GNP, the ratio of dependence on bond issues in the annual budget of the central government, and the ratio of the service cost to outstanding debt are all high in Japan compared with other advanced countries. The Ministry of Finance sticks to the principle of sound finance and is eager to reduce the volume of bond issues. However, the high savings ratio in Japan causes a surplus in the current account in the balance of international payments. In order for the national economy as a whole to be balanced, a certain level of bond issues by the government seems desirable.

Past experiences could be categorized into three patterns, none of which is appropriate for the future. In the 1960's, the government budget was in equilibrium. Private investment was so brisk that it absorbed fully private savings. During the first half of the 1980's, a restrictive fiscal policy was imposed. This restrictive fiscal policy might have been a precondition for a successful administrative reform executed at the same time. However, it cannot be denied that the same restrictive fiscal policy brought about slow economic growth at home. In 1986 and 1987, active fiscal measures were introduced. The fiscal deficit was narrowed.

The Establishment of Financial Stability

The dollar fell sharply in the spring of 1987 and again toward the end of the year. The rates of interest rose in the summer preceding the October stock market crash. Volatility in the asset market worldwide threatened the stability of the world economy. Given the imbalances in the current accounts among major countries, financial instability may continue to be a problem for economic management. Policy coordination of the leading countries, particularly monetary cooperation, seems to be a popular issue. To avoid financial crises, monetary authorities should act wisely and preferably in a cooperative way. Central bankers acted wisely after the October crash, as they did in the fall of 1982 when Mexico's debt repayment ran into trouble. Cooperative action in such cases is desirable and necessary. Also, the major nations should cooperate in sharing the cost of "international public goods" such as defense of the Western alliance, development aid, basic research, and so on. These must not be the sole responsibility of the United States. Japan should contribute more.

The misalignment of exchange rates in the mid-80's has disappeared. This also promotes the feasibility of exchange rate stabilization. However, as mentioned above, imbalances in current accounts among major nations remain large. It seems premature to fix exchange rates at the current level. Given the fundamental disequilibrium, official targeting of exchange rates may only help speculators. Financial flexibility has its own merits, particularly in an age of uncertainty. Volatility in interest rates, apparently amplified by the recent liberalization and internationalization of financial markets may be working as a stabilizing factor for the economy. Whenever one senses approaching inflation, interest rates will rise so as to suppress the threat of inflation.

The Fight Against Protectionist Legislation

The responsibility to promote free trade is with the surplus countries. Japan should continue to open its agricultural, construction, and other markets. This may serve the purpose of rationalizing Japanese agriculture, construction, and other industries. Today, U.S. unemployment is a low six percent and there is no longer any alarm that imports are taking away American jobs. In fact, there is the opposite fear. Reducing imports while aggregate demand remains unabated sparks inflation. Protectionists are fighting the war of the past.

What is and is not fair is not always clear. Some regard, for example, sales at prices under cost as unfair. However, suppose that cost can be reduced as output is increased, and suppose that demand will expand significantly as the price is lowered. Under such circumstances, is it fair or unfair for firms to set price below the current cost in expectation that the future cost will be reduced as a result of the expansion of demand and output? This is not the case of predatory pricing. If cost reduction can be duly expected, many firms can enter the market. They can raise money to finance a temporary deficit by persuading capitalists of expected cost reduction and profit in the future as long as the capital market is perfect and sufficiently farsighted. Cost must be covered. But in what time-span?

Similarly, is it Japan's having an industrial policy or America's not having one that is to be criticized? Or is it just to have recession cartels as in Japan or not to have them as in the U.S.? It is only natural that there should be disagreement, both in Japan and in the U.S., over which system is better. The pitfalls of arguing fair trade is that the advocates are all too prone to close their eyes to these complexities and to draw a simple contrast between virtue and villainy. Criticizing trade partners as unfair may gradually erode the basis of mutual respect and friendship. Psychological and political costs cannot be overlooked.

All of this is to suggest that the politics of economic policies and the wisdom of economic strategies must be better understood in Japan and the U.S. so that policies for the future, especially the early 1990s, can be successful and productive.

YUTAKA KOSAI
President, Japan Economic Research Center. Previously Professor, Tokyo Institute of Technology 1981-1987. General Senior Research Officer, Economic Research Institute, Economic Planning Agency (EPA). Publications include, The Era of High-Speed Growth, *University of Tokyo Press, 1986, and* The Contemporary Japanese Economy, *Macmillan, 1984.*

Japanese-American Defense Policies for a Post-Reagan Era

John Endicott

In late 1987, Japan experienced a transition of executive authority from one prime minister to another, and very shortly the United States will have a new president. What will be the policy impact? Will the transition to new leadership in both governments presage changes in course, or does a large enough consensus exist at all levels to ensure a smooth transition? This paper will examine the likely course of the U.S.-Japan security relationship with a focus on Japanese defense policy in the years ahead. Overall, evolutionary developments will prevail with the next U.S. administration, but some realignment within the ruling Liberal Democratic Party (LDP) on defense issues may evolve in this process. The political alliance in Japan that has existed within the LDP on defense issues may show signs of deterioration under pressures of economic restructuring, internationalization, and growing doubts about the U.S. security guarantee, including its nuclear dimension. And there are new questions about the seriousness of the "Red threat."[1]

Economic and security issues have always been linked. The inconsistencies of a security policy that admits of complete dependence on the United States for nuclear security, but insists on an autonomous agricultural base in the name of "national security" should be clarified. The interrelationship of security and economic policy assures that the number of crosscutting forces in the U.S.-Japanese security relationship will grow.

It is also likely that managing the relationship will become more, rather than less, complex. This being the case, professionals on both sides must become more outspoken and exercise leadership to strengthen ties.

Background Issues

As a result of the defeat in the Pacific War, Japanese postwar leaders realized that two basic policy lines were necessary for the future success and development of their recovering country: one was the absolute necessity to minimize the economic drain imposed by standing military forces; and the second was the obvious need for a close working security relationship with the United States. Prime Minister Shigeru Yoshida recognized both; he led Japan into the United States-Japan Security Treaty of 1952, which was followed in 1954 by the concept of "balanced defense," placing scarce economic resources in economic development programs, not into defense. The creation of a small defense force that could be expanded if "real" threats materialized was also endorsed. Pressures of the moment for Japanese rearmament were rejected as being out of line with the 1947 Peace Constitution, as well as unacceptable to the Japanese body politic which was war weary and unconvinced about the virtue of military power.

The first significant change in the U.S.-Japan bilateral security relationship occurred in 1960, when the 1952 treaty was replaced with a revised agreement, the Treaty of Mutual Cooperation and Security. This document fundamentally changed the relationship limiting U.S. rights to use Japan-based facilities and requiring that major force level changes be introduced into Japan only after prior consultation with the Japanese government. Calling for U.S. and Japan to react to attacks against Japanese territory, it did not introduce a reciprocal obligation on the part of Japan to come to the aid of the United States. In 1960 no one could realistically conceive of such a scenario.

These changes were not received with a great deal of enthusiasm by the Japanese people. The resistance power of the Left, opposition political parties and labor unions movements was brought to bear against the Kishi Cabinet in 1960, and Japan experienced one of its greatest periods of internal disruption, even more intense than the May Day riots of the 1950s. When the treaty was signed, Kishi resigned and turned over the government to another Liberal Democratic leader, Hayato Ikeda, who returned to the economic policies of the Yoshida era and concentrated the nation on an income doubling plan for Japan—not a military budget expansion.[2]

While the new emphasis was on economic development, the

period from 1958 to 1976 was still an era of significant rebuilding of the Japanese Self Defense Forces (JSDF). Four five-year defense build-up plans had been completed but, as the fifth was being reviewed, significant political opposition developed causing a new approach. In 1976, this plan was introduced and endorsed by Takeo Miki who became prime minister in the wake of the Lockheed scandal when Prime Minister Kakuei Tanaka was forced to step down. Sensitive to the political Left and responsive to an international environment of detente, Miki led the LDP to accept a framework of defense-related policy decisions that today remain a central part of the subsequent political scene. The main contribution of the Miki era was the creation of the National Defense Program Outline (*Taiko*) that established overall force structure levels and organizational objectives for the Japan Self Defense Forces. These levels were intended to remain in force until conditions changed in Asia that would warrant reconsideration. Further, to mollify the opposition and put a cap on military expenditures, a one percent of GNP ceiling was placed on Japan Defense Agency (JDA) budgets. Japan also reaffirmed its policy not to export weapons. Through very active political involvement, Miki was able to get the Parliament (Diet) to ratify the non-proliferation treaty that had been signed in 1970 and to reassert Japan's three non-nuclear principles: not to produce, import, or allow the stationing of nuclear weapons in Japan. While not accomplished during 1976, Miki did initiate talks in that year that led to the 1978 U.S.-Japan Guidelines for Defense Cooperation, establishing a new base-line for the defense discussions.

With the Reagan administration in 1981, the Japanese prime minister at that time, Zenko Suzuki, committed Japan to a new level of active participation. He pledged that Japan, "within the framework of the Constitution" could protect its air and sea lanes out to 1000 miles.[3] This statement went far in addressing the increasing criticism arising from the U.S. Congress regarding the notion of a Japanese lack of contribution to or "free ride" on defense.

Prime Minister Yasuhiro Nakasone signaled a new era in Japanese political style. He peppered his speeches with phrases like "braving the storm," "dawning of a new era," and the all important word, *kokusaika* or internationalization, which took on new meanings under his leadership. Nakasone also changed the political consultative mode by turning to the frequent use of ad hoc advisory groups that allowed him to circumvent political party and government policy formulation bureaucracies and appeal directly to the people. He practiced top-down politics. Keen on action, he indicated to the world that he was not a one-issue man. He visited South Korea, sang Korean songs—in Korean—and solved a sticky multi-billion dollar aid issue.

His second major international initiative was a journey to the United States to establish a personalized "Ron-Yasu" relationship with the U.S. president. It was also the moment of the *Washington Post's* quote (or misquote) of Nakasone that Japan was an unsinkable aircraft carrier and Soviet foreign minister, Andre Gromyko's musings about "big targets in a nuclear weapons era." Nakasone went on during the course of the next five years, to expand the Japanese national consensus on more open discussions of defense and security issues. Through the report of an ad hoc commission headed by Kyoto University professor, Masataka Kosaka, Nakasone included, in ways previously unaccomplished, a wider group of non-defense opinion leaders in security debates. The "Kosaka Report" called on the Japanese to treat the defense issue in a more realistic manner, stressing strategic and mission concerns. It even called upon the government to reexamine some long-held planning constraints, such as the one percent of GNP barrier and the National Defense Program Outline (*Taiko*), and even touched upon the subject of the three non-nuclear principles.

Another ad hoc commission during Prime Minister Nakasone's tenure was headed by Toshio Doko of the Japan Federation of Economic Organizations (*Keidanren*). It called for administrative reforms necessary to streamline the Japanese decision-making system and government for the 21st century. The Defense Agency was included in this review as well as the sub-cabinet-level advisory body, the National Defense Council. The Cabinet Secretariat also came in for comment, and some reorganization, to facilitate the coordination of government-wide decisions when sensitive security matters were involved.

Other major accomplishments of the Nakasone Era that contributed to the increased security awareness and defense capability of Japan included: Nakasone's 1983 promise to block the three northern straits in a national emergency, and his signing of the joint communique at the Williamsburg Summit that committed him—and Japan—to the notion that the defense of freedom and justice of democracies would require the maintenance of "sufficient military strength to deter any attack, to counter any threat and ensure the peace;"[4] the Japanese agreement to join in the joint research phase of the U.S. SDI project; the announcement to finance a precision navigation system for ships in the Persian Gulf; the decision to jointly develop with the United States the replacement support fighter for the F-1, the FSX; the decision to redefine defense budget allocations (tying them to total five-year funding for mid-term plans rather than strictly one percent of the GNP); the completion of the base-support program for the location of two U.S. F-16 squadrons in northern Honshu; continuing close military exercise relationships between U.S. and Japanese defense forces on the sea, ground, and in the air; a public commitment to positively share in the burden imposed on U.S. naval resources by the continuing Iran-Iraq War in the Persian Gulf; and, in October 1987, the recommendation of the Ground Defense Posture for the 21st Century Study Group that "the Ground Self Defense Force should shift its strategy from Inland Persistent Defense to Forward Attack and Early Breakthrough."[5] This last item was, in essence, an outgrowth of his earlier decision to pursue a defense concept that extended Japan's defense perimeter to a "stand-off ocean defense of the archipelago."[6]

Of special significance during the Nakasone era was his determined support to place the five-year planning documents of the Japan Defense Agency on a stronger bureaucratic footing. Even though an attempt to remove the one percent GNP barrier failed in 1985, he was successful in changing the status of the five-year mid-term defense plans to be official government policy. Henceforth, JDA five-year plans were supported by the Cabinet. The 1986-1990 Mid-Term Defense Estimate, approved in 1985, thus became a major government program or plan leading to the attainment of the kind of defense capabilities necessary for a stand-off ocean defense of Japan. This plan provides for the following additions to Japanese defense capabilities.

For air defense:

- increasing the number of modern front-line F-15 fighter interceptors (the most modern aircraft flown by the U.S. Air Force) to 200;
- modernizing the approximately 100 F-4 "Phantom" interceptors, thus providing Japan with a total of 300 capable tactical fighters (200 F-15s plus 100 F-4s), about the number the U.S. has defending the continental U.S.;
- research on the acquisition of tanker aircraft to increase the effectiveness of the 300 interceptors and air to surface fighters Japan will have in the 1990s;
- replacement of the surface-to-air "Nike-J" missiles with the U.S. Army's modern "Patriot" system;
- research of an extremely long-range over-the-horizon (OTH) radar system capable of early detection of aircraft operating in a broad area of Soviet Far Eastern air space;
- acquisition of additional short-range, early-warning aircraft capable of detecting low-flying aircraft such as the Soviet MIG-25 which landed in Hokkaido without detection in 1976.

For sea defense:
- increasing the number of destroyer-type surface ships from 50 to 60, almost three times as many as the U.S. Seventh Fleet which has responsibilities for the entire Western Pacific and Indian Oceans;
- acquiring two guided missile destroyer-type ships with the U.S. Navy's state-of-the art "Aegis" air defense system; and
- doubling the number of modern U.S. P-3C anti-submarine warfare (ASW) aircraft, bringing the total to 100, about four times as many as in the U.S. Seventh Fleet.[7]

For land defense:
- Upgrading the capability of the Ground Self Defense Forces will be realized in this 1986-90 plan through the acquisition of new tanks and U.S. anti-tank helicopters, concentrating ammunition in Hokkaido, obtaining new surface-to-surface missiles, and redeploying some front-line ground units to Hokkaido.

According to some U.S. defense officials, the completion of this five-year plan will provide Japan with the "minimum level of capability necessary to meet the 1981 defense goals announced by Prime Minister Suzuki."[8] However, Prime Minister Nakasone will get the credit, as it was his initiative that enhanced the plan's status and permitted expenditures over one percent of the GNP to be spent to attain the goals.

Prime Minister Takeshita's Agenda

Nakasone stepped down in November 1987 to continue his role as a faction leader in the Diet, and to form his International Institute for Global Peace, a "strategy formulation organ for Japan's diplomacy."[9] The man who inherited these responsibilities as president of the Liberal Democratic Party and as prime minister of the Government was Noboru Takeshita. During the extensive press coverage of last November, it became clear that Takeshita, while standing for policies that would create an "open culture and economic state," would, in large measure, continue the security policy associated with Nakasone.

Takeshita stressed as main pillars of his overall programs:
- Increased imports
- The promotion of cultural diplomacy
- Upholding U.S.-Japanese security cooperation
- Supporting U.S.-Soviet arms control efforts

John Endicott

Takeshita brought to the national arena the concept of *furusato*—the "my hometown" idea. This policy captured his interest and emphasis on domestic programs. Generally, *furusato* embodies the ideas of:
- Rectifying high density living conditions
- Relocating one function from each ministry and agency to outside Tokyo
- Eliminating speculative land transactions
- Establishing nationwide information networks
- Coordinating the development of industry, technology and culture.

As a former Finance Minister, Takeshita voiced concern with the 18.4 trillion yen amount for the mid-term defense build-up for 1986-1990, but emphasized that Japan should play a wider role in contributing to world peace through economic and cultural cooperation. Overall, his leadership style is characterized as one stressing consensus and "listening to real intentions."

Typically, American observers—and some Japanese—wondered if such leadership characteristics and policy inclinations would support the needs of a successful prime minister. A representative U.S. observation was:

> ...However well intentioned, Mr. Takeshita will take the more traditional route in resolving problems; namely, when trouble appears, he will prefer to temporize in the hope the problem will subside....[10]

After almost a year in power, Takeshita has demonstrated considerable leadership. On defense, the next U.S. administration will find Takeshita and the Japanese government dealing with certain limits as defined in Article 9 of the Constitution which clearly proscribes the maintenance of "...land, sea, and air forces, as well as other war potential..." and refuses to recognize the right of belligerency of the state. Of almost equal significance are the defense policy constraints that were established during the government of Takeo Miki: the National Defense Program Outline (*Taiko*), the one percent of GNP ceiling on defense expenditures, the rearticulation of the Three Non-nuclear Principles, the ratification of the NPT, confirmation of the Principles of Non-export of Weapons, and the beginning of U.S.-Japanese bilateral talks leading to the achievement of the Guidelines for U.S.-Japanese Defense Cooperation of 1978. This complex policy framework (now more than a decade old) warrants review as it will likely set the tone of the first four-year term of the next U.S. president.

The National Defense Program Outline still serves as the basic force structure guide for the Japan Self Defense Forces. Equipment levels specified in the Outline will probably be completely reached sometime in 1992. The force structure identified in the '76 *Taiko* will be attained during Takeshita's tenure. And, if one assumes that the current prime minister will serve two terms as president of the LDP, that is until November 1991, the primary force structure envisaged in the *Taiko* will be that of the Takeshita administration.

The broad outlines for the next mid-term defense plan taking Japan into the mid-1990s have reportedly been decided. Press accounts indicate that the primary objectives will be "at improving the ground defense capability of Self-Defense Forces in Japan's northernmost...island of Hokkaido...,"[11] and generally aim to continue to stress the modernization of air and naval interdiction capabilities. Such items as long-range airborne warning and control system (AWACS) aircraft, increased "Aegis"-type naval vessels, multiple launch rocket systems (MLRS), hardened shelters, and better command and control facilities may be in the new plan.

The second item is the one percent GNP defense increase ceiling; recently of major interest due to its redefinition in 1987. While the one percent ceiling was exceeded last year with 1.004% being realized, the one percent barrier continues to play a role as an invisible, non-official benchmark against which the world and many Japanese measure increases in defense expenditures. Currently, the defense budget is seen in terms of a total amount needed to meet the needs of a five-year mid-term defense plan. Civilian control, of course, is exercised in the guidance for the plan, approval of the overall concept, and through the yearly budgetary process. In January 1987, a total defense spending limit for 1986-1990 was set at 18.4 trillion yen. The budget outlay for FY 88 (beginning 1 April) will be 3,700.3 billion yen—an increase of 5.2% over last year. This amounts to 1.013% of the projected GNP and includes such banner items as initial costs for a 7,200 ton "Aegis"-type missile ship, developmental funds for the FSX support fighter, geographical research needed for an over-the-horizon (OTH) radar on Iwo Jima, an anti-submarine warfare center at Yokosuka, and continuing procurement of the F-15J fighters. Of special interest was the 79.2 billion yen for improvements in U.S. military facilities in Japan and 41.1 billion yen for labor costs for 21,000 Japanese workers.[12] Such expenditures and the willingness to offset in some manner the U.S. costs for patrolling the Persian Gulf, should be welcomed by the next U.S. administration interested in an enhanced Japanese defense capabilities that also reflects support for U.S. out-of-area security commitments.

The third category still very much a part of the Japanese defense policy environment is the Three Non-nuclear Principles and membership in the NPT. Japan's unique role in the world as an advocate of nuclear disarmament has been reaffirmed by its very strong endorsement of the U.S.-Soviet INF Treaty which removes SS-20s from the Soviet Far East nuclear inventories. Continued Japanese support for U.S. arms control initiatives with the Soviet Union should be sought by a post-Reagan administration.

The fourth element is the Three Principles of Non-export of Weapons (not to export weapons to countries engaged in hostilities, about to be, or on a United Nations list). This has been maintained, with the exception of a Japanese agreement to provide certain weapons technology to the U.S., under terms of the U.S.-Japan Security Agreement. While this holds more in the way of promise than accomplishments, it does represent the basis on which to build an increasing close defense relationship. The Takeshita government moved, during the visit by the Prime Minister to Washington in January 1988, to assure greater progress in this area. The recent agreement to co-develop the FSX will be held up as a model for future U.S.-Japanese efforts at co-development. There are some Japanese defense accomplishments in image-homing missile technology, for example, that are very impressive. Whether such an item could become a prospect for co-development should be further studied.

The final 1976-based defense planning factor led to the 1978 Guidelines for U.S.-Japanese Defense Cooperation. Over the ten years since the Guidelines were articulated, defense cooperation has continuously become more practical, involving joint exercises, and has of late, entered the area of a joint study group to consider requirements to airlift U.S. forces and equipment to Japan in an emergency.[13] Efforts, such as the one just mentioned, indicate a willingness on the part of the Japanese government to continue with developments to perfect a joint U.S.-Japanese capability for the defense of Japan. The completion of the study and the active encouragement of continued U.S.-Japanese exercises should be of keen interest to any new U.S. administration.

With regard to the Opposition Parties in the Diet, they are not a major factor. However, one can point to their roles as: guardians of Article 9 of the Constitution (their agreement is practically necessary for any change, in light of the method for constitutional revision) and participants in the Diet budget review process where they actively carry out interpellation of government officials. Recently, they held up Budget Committee deliberations for days by taking exception to Prime Minister Takeshita's position on U.S. respect for Japan's Three Non-nuclear Principles. It is clear that the role for the next U.S. administration regarding Japanese opposition parties should be exactly as it is now: offering to brief visiting dignitaries on U.S. perceptions of U.S.-Japanese bilateral interests so that their continued evolution away from policies such as "unarmed neutrality" might be encouraged.

In a major recent development the Japan Socialist Party (JSP) announced a willingness to acquiesce in the reality of the JSDF in order to make alignment or union with the Komeito (Clean Government Party) possible. This event, plus the continuing saga of labor union realignment and reorganization in Japan, indicates a likely new correlation of political forces among the opposition during Prime Minister Takeshita's tenure. Whether a more consolidated opposition will equate to a more efficient one is another question. In defense terms, however, it does mean that as long as Takeshita continues on an evolutionary path, opposition acquiescence can be expected. Such a path should be encouraged by the next U.S. president.

With respect to the general population and the support Prime Minister Takeshita will or will not have the next administration must consider that there has been a general trend in opinion polling data that reveals substantial Japanese public support for the notion of a larger, more involved role for Japan in the world. However, it has consistently been accompanied by indications that this larger role not be in the military sphere. (Generally, polls reveal 60% or more of respondents oppose any increase in defense spending or size of the JSDF.)

Americans must be mindful of the increasing impact of generational change and the general aging of the senior Japanese leadership. Of interest to future U.S. administrations will be the developing attitudes and impact on the Japanese defense scene of the so-called *Shinjinrui* or "new human beings." What will be the long-term affect of these new lifestyles that increasingly question many of the traditional reciprocal values long held in Japan? Admittedly, the ultimate impact of the *Shinjinrui* phenomenon will not be manifest until post-Takeshita (and, therefore, well beyond post-Reagan), if not well into the 21st century. Whether these young people will be mobilized politically or remain apolitical and hedonistic will have a large influence on Japan's defense policy of the future, and should be worthy of continuing interest by us all.

With this as background, it is possible to see the Japanese defense environment that will greet the incoming U.S. administration and to observe some of the areas of possible consultation for the new U.S. and Japanese governments. All the 1976 methods for delimiting defense are still in effect, but all have changed. The accent and nuance for defense in Japan has changed; on the one hand presenting Prime Minister Takeshita with certain constraints, but on the other, creating opportunities much different from those of 1976.

John Endicott

The Post-Reagan Era

One thing to stress is the pro-active nature of the first months of the Takeshita government in areas related to Japan's Asian defense or security role. In the first 90 days, the new prime minister attended the ASEAN Summit in Manila, and announced a two billion dollar aid program oriented to a further realization of the positive involvement of Japan in Southeast Asia (envisaged by Fukuda some years ago in the Fukuda Doctrine). While the defense side of the aid will be in all likelihood next to zero, the "security" impact will be significant. This point was made earlier in Seizaburo Sato's paper.

During bilateral talks with President Reagan in January, Takeshita, on defense-related issues, focused on economic measures to give greater support to U.S. forces in Japan; announced that Japan would pay the entire cost of eight specific allowances for Japanese employees on U.S. bases; agreed to initiate a joint U.S.-Japanese study for the airlifting of troops and equipment to Japan in the event of an emergency; and put new stress, as mentioned above, on the FSX co-development project as a hallmark project for future cooperation.

His stance regarding international terrorism was strident, and on January 26, in response to the North Korean bombing of a South Korean jetliner over Burma, his cabinet secretary "strongly denounced" the North Korean act and outlined retaliatory measures that Japan would immediately impose. Takeshita also made a special effort to insure that the new Korean leader, Roh Tae Woo, knew of his interest in working closely with South Korea during his administration. He announced plans to attend the inauguration of the new Korean President and did so.

In December, while most of the world focused on General Secretary Gorbachev's visit to Washington, Japanese Air Defense Forces in Okinawa fired on an intruding Soviet TU-16 bomber. The Takeshita government followed the incident with a strong protest for the blatant disregard for Japanese airspace and noted with alarm that the intruding aircraft recovered at a Pyongyang airfield before flying on to the Soviet Union. This marked the first time since the war that a Japanese aircraft fired at an intercepted aircraft. The Soviets later apologized.

Prime Minister Takeshita, himself, caused the Japan Socialist Party to symbolically boycott sessions of the Diet budgetary committee when he held fast to his government's position on U.S. observance of the Three Non-nuclear Principles. When he opened the Diet Session of 25 January, he and part of his national security team, Foreign Minister Uno, Finance Minister Miyazawa, and Economic Planning Agency Director Nakao, made a clear statement on Japanese security policy. Takeshita's goal was to "maximize

Pacific Forum

Japan's global economic, diplomatic and security affairs."[14] This new assertiveness has implications for Americans dealing with Japan. Expectations and performance have changed.

It is already clear that Prime Minister Takeshita will seek continued close development of the U.S.-Japanese defense and security relationship. Within this context, however, there will be a gradual intrusion of the tensions of the bilateral economic and trade relationship. The Toshiba technology leak case, FSX development, the Fujitsu-Fairchild ownership case, the LE-5 rocket engine technology transfer refusal, "Aegis" missile system sensitivities, and the Glenn Amendment (related to SDI contracts) underline the increasing complexities of the bilateral relationship and the need for professionalism on both sides.

Gone also are the days when technology transfer can be accepted as a one-way street. A brief examination of selected items of Japanese research and development demonstrate the potential of a two-way exchange. To a project like the FSX might be added the mine-laying system for C-130s, a control system for a new helicopter rotor hub, research for a high-temperature turbine, and other projects of the JDA's Technical Research and Development Institute.[15] Viewing tech-transfer and co-development in terms of greater support for U.S. forces, Prime Minister Takeshita and his Director General of the Defense Agency could assure an increasingly active bilateral relationship in a critical era of relative fiscal constraint and needed military reform.

A new U.S. administration might also propose to the Takeshita government that an enhanced system of exchange between government-sponsored policy oriented think tanks be examined. The new Nakasone International Institute for Global Peace and the proposed Foreign Ministry-sponsored think tank that will focus on security issues might begin their respective endeavors by inviting U.S. representatives from the Center for the Study of Foreign Affairs of the U.S. State Department and from the Institute for National Strategic Studies of the Department of Defense. Exchanges of private citizens knowledgeable in these areas should also be encouraged, such as seen in meetings of the Pacific Forum.

Of equal importance to the U.S.-Japan relationship from a global perspective are Japan's defense ties with the rest of Asia. Of greatest concern to Japan's neighbors is the legacy of the 1930s—which is 50 years past but seems like yesterday to many. However, the emphasis must be placed on the future, not the past. The changes that have occurred to the Japanese political system, society, and even culture assure us that the Japan of 1930 has been replaced by a democratic, polycentric society of contesting interest groups. Prime Minister Takeshita stated in his January 25 policy speech, that Japan will not become a military power. In so speaking, he reflects political reality—not just an expedient political position. Japan's contribution to the defense of Asia, he maintains, will be made through political influence and economic power. A complete and genuine understanding of this development is keen to any new U.S. administration. U.S. policies that push Japan toward greater reliance on military developments, for example, offensive capabilities such as aircraft carriers,[16] tactical nuclear weapons, and systems that support power projection capabilities, would risk major political dislocations domestically and regionally.

Already, Japan's Foreign Minister is committed to greater official development aid (ODA), a more active foreign policy, and the internationalization of Japanese society.[17] By achieving Japan's defense objectives—the defense of Japan from regional conventional threats—Japan will contribute to the security of Asia by providing a secure foundation for greater economic and trade involvement with all its neighbors.

As we view the Takeshita and the post-Reagan eras, one must be realistic and recognize that the defense policy of Japan will be largely absorbed into the U.S.-Japanese bilateral relationship but her security policy, that which includes active trade, increased ODA, and the opening of Japanese markets to all competitive producers, will involve all the nations of the Pacific Rim. At this point, one can only echo the call made by the United States Congress that encourages Japan to realize its global power status by contributing three percent of its GNP as ODA by 1992.

There are two additional critical priorities for the next U.S. administration: the encouragement of continued progress toward accomplishing the Japanese defense goals already established for 1990 and the achievement of significant increases of ODA by 1992. This could mean that as much as 90 billion dollars of development aid could be made available to the international system. (Fifty billion have already been pledged by the Takeshita government.) The impact on the Third World system would be dramatic. However, the administration of such an amount would immediately overburden the international developmental community. Its security implications are equally impressive. It would be the equivalent in 1988 dollars of several Marshall Plans every year. It would permit, for example, the funding of the Philippine land redistribution program, a canal through the Kra Isthmus, major Latin American programs, and much more.

There are constraints. Levels of ODA significantly higher than those currently provided by Japan could have a major security impact throughout the world, but the Japanese government today does not have access to the necessary funds. Taxation reforms would be necessary. Three percent of GNP may seem far away and unrealistic at first glance, but such a contribution would only bring the total, comprehensive Japanese burden for the security of the international system to approximately 4.1 percent. Contrasted to other members of the OECD, Japan's present one percent for defense is embarrassing. As Japan sets out to seriously debate the merits of possessing "...defense capabilities commensurate with our national power," her major developmental role should be kept in mind.[18]

Overall, the positive trends in Japan are encouraging. The task for the post-Reagan era is to build on these trends, seek to influence the total package of Japan's contributions to global security while not moving Japan's offensive military capacity beyond its domestic constitutional limits or its global needs.

JOHN ENDICOTT
USAF Ret., Director, Institute for National Strategic Studies, National Defense University, Washington, D.C. Previously Head of the Research Directorate, National Defense University; Associate Dean of the National War College for Faculty and Academic Programs. He also served as the Deputy Air Force Representative to the Military Staff Committee of the United Nations. Publications: Japan's Nuclear Option, The Politics of East Asia, *and* American Defense Policy. *Graduate of Ohio State, cum laude; Ph.D. from the Fletcher School of Law and Diplomacy.*

Endnotes

1. See especially the article by Takehito Seki in the December 1987 edition of *Sekai*, pages 71-84.
2. For an excellent account of the role of the Socialist opposition during this period refer to Allan B. Cole, et al, *Socialist Parties in Postwar Japan*, (New Haven, CT: Yale University Press, 1966).
3. See especially, James E. Auer, "The Global Influence of Japanese Defense Efforts," unpublished paper, March 24, 1988.
4. "Statement at Williamsburg of Seven Summit Countries," May 29, 1983.
5. Mitsutake Sato, unpublished paper, "U.S.-Japan Security Relationship," March 2, 1988, p. 12.
6. Auer, p. 13.
7. Auer, p. 14.
8. Auer, p. 15.
9. *Nihon Keizai Shimbun*, October 27, 1987, p. 2.
10. *Japan Economic Survey*, January 1988, p. 15.
11. *Foreign Broadcast Information Service* (FBIS), EAS-88-020, February 1, 1988, p. 4.
12. *FBIS*, EAS-87-248, December 28, 1987.
13. *The Daily Yomiuri*, January 29, 1988, p. 1.
14. *Japan Economic Institute Report*, No. 5B, p. 7.
15. *Aerospace-Japan Weekly*, No. 852, pp. 3-4.
16. See the *Yomiuri Shimbun*, December 18, 1987 for reference to light aircraft carrier for Japan.
17. *Japan Economic Institute Report*, No. 5B, p. 7.
18. Associated Press quoting Prime Minister Takeshita speaking before the March 21st graduating class of the Japanese National Defense Academy, *Washington Times*, March 22, 1988, p. 6.

Committee Participants

Japanese-American Study Committee on Comprehensive Security

John Endicott,
Director, Institute for National Strategic Studies, National Defense University

Philip C. Habib,
Former U.S. Undersecretary of State; recent Presidential envoy to the Middle East, Central America; Chairman of the Board, Pacific Forum

Tsuyoshi Hasegawa,
Professor, Slavic Research Center, Hokkaido University

Thomas B. Hayward,
Former Chief of U.S. Naval Operations and Member of the Joint Chiefs of Staff; Vice Chairman of the Board, Pacific Forum

John H. Holdridge,
Former U.S. Assistant Secretary of State for East Asia and the Pacific, and Ambassador to Indonesia; Board Member, Pacific Forum

Yutaka Kosai,
President, Japan Economic Research Center

Edward Lincoln,
Senior Fellow, The Brookings Institution

Makoto Momoi,
Guest Research Fellow, The Yomiuri Research Institute

Ronald A. Morse,
Development Officer, The Library of Congress

Daniel O'Donohue,
Principal Deputy Director, Policy Planning Staff, U.S. Department of State

Pacific Forum

Yoshio Okawara,
Executive Advisor, Japan Federation of Economic Organizations; Advisor to Ministry of Foreign Affairs, Japan; Former Ambassador to the United States; Board Member, Pacific Forum

Seizaburo Sato,
Professor of Political Science, The University of Tokyo; Member of several Prime Ministerial commissions; Member, Research Council, Pacific Forum

Robert A. Scalapino,
Director, Institute of East Asian Studies, University of California, Berkeley; Robson Research Professor of Government; Board Member, Pacific Forum

Heizo Takenaka,
Associate Professor, Faculty of Economics, Osaka University

Akihiko Tanaka,
Associate Professor, Department of Social and International Relations, The University of Tokyo

Lloyd R. Vasey,
President, Pacific Forum